Let The Bible Speak ...
About Tongues

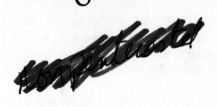

AN EXPOSITION AND AN EXPLANATION

BY RICHARD C. SCHWAB

Let the Bible *Speak* . . . About Tongues
Copyright © 1983 by Richard C. Schwab
Vancouver, Washington 98661

Printed in the United States of America

First Printing, 1983

ISBN

Herren Printing Co.
2009 East Burnside
Portland, Oregon 97214

Table of Contents

MAP AND GRAPH

Dedication

to my faithful wife and companion, Eleanor,
and to the glory of God!

Acknowledgements

Mrs. Marilyn McGinnis of Glendale, California, journalist and author, for her encouragement and help.

Miss Ann Staatz of Seattle, Washington, for her wise counsel and editorial comments.

Mr. Donald W. Patten, author and editor of Pacific Meridian Publishing Company, for sound direction and editing review.

My wife Eleanor for her countless hours of manuscript typing, review, and positive contribution.

To these my special thanks. They have given much in the preparation of this book.

Foreword

I consider it a distinct privilege to write a foreword for Richard Schwab's book, *"Let the Bible Speak . . . About Tongues."* I have made an intensive effort to keep up with the literature written on this subject over the last 20 plus years. I believe that I have read most of the books that have been written on the subject and I can say without hesitation that Pastor Schwab's work, written over a period of five years, represents the finest balance of careful scholarship and practical application that I have seen on the subject. In fact, as I finished a very careful review of the manuscript, I found myself saying, "That's a book that I would have been happy to have authored."

Not only is Pastor Schwab's work a fine demonstration of careful and relevant exposition of the Scripture, but it is a manifestation of the fruit of the Spirit in its presentation. A work on such a controversial subject as this could easily degenerate into a caustic polemic, but such is not the case. Pastor Schwab really seeks to exercise kindness with conviction. I believe he has accomplished in large measure the Pauline exhortation to speak the truth in love. If I were to pick one book to give to a person to read on this subject, this is the book I would pick.

> Earl D. Radmacher, *president*
> Western Conservative Baptist Seminary
> Portland, Oregon

"Wherefore, tongues are for a sign . . ." (I Cor. 14:22a)
of the baptism of the Holy Spirit?
or to the unbelieving of Israel.

Introduction

The modern tongues movement is spreading around the globe like "wildfire across the prairie". People everywhere are asking questions about it. How does the phenomenon relate to Biblical tongues? Should the Christian seek to speak in tongues? What are the immediate and long-range effects of speaking in tongues?

In the following I propose to combine an *exposition* of the major passages in the Bible and an *explanation* of the related issues to help answer these and other questions.

No attempt has been made to bring exhaustive exegetical study but rather to offer truth simply so that the average Christian can understand the Scriptural gift of tongues and present-day glossolalia.

I have sought balance in the presentation of a subject often discussed without balance.

To you of sincere heart, desiring to know truth on the authority of the Word of God, this book should be of practical help.

I strongly urge you to read the appropriate Scripture before the consideration of each chapter, then to keep that Bible passage open before you for continual reference.

The King James Version has been used throughout unless otherwise designated.

This brief volume is presented with the prayer that the Holy Spirit, faithful in inspiration of the Scripture, would illuminate mind and heart according to His will.

CHAPTER ONE

Historical Sketch

Biblical Scope

In the beginning mankind spoke one language, or tongue. "And the whole earth was of one language, and of one speech," (Gen. 11:1). The Lord Himself verified this fact, "Behold, the people is one, and they have all one language . . .," (Gen. 11:6a).

After the flood and man's failure under the Noahic Covenant, God brought judgment upon the children of Shem, Ham, and Japheth, Noah's sons. This happened in the land of Shinar, Babylonia, at the tower of Babel. There God said, "Go to, let us go down, and there confound their language, that they may not understand one another's speech. So the Lord scattered them abroad from thence upon the face of all the earth . . .," (Gen. 11:7-8).

God thwarted man's proud assumption of power and might at Babel by changing his original one language into the many languages of the subsequent peoples of all the earth. This condition exists down to the present day.

Tongues in the Old Testament

Though the Old Testament may contain several veiled references to tongues under the broad meaning of "prophesying" (as I Kings 18:29; Jer. 29:26; I Sam. 10:6, 10), there is no explicit reference to tongues speaking.

Tongues in the New Testament

The New Testament, however, reveals the genuine gift of tongues as the God-given ability to speak actual languages. Pertinent passages in Acts (2:1-21; 10:44-48; with 11:15-18; 19:1-7), and in I Corinthians (12:1-14:40), also in Mark (16:15-20), will be discussed in the remaining chapters of this book. No other references to a tongues experience appear later than those in Ephesus (Acts 19) and in Corinth about A.D. 55.

Ancient Occurrences

Secular records reveal that tongues speaking occurred in pagan cultures before the day of Pentecost.

James B. Pritchard in his book, *Ancient Near Eastern Texts*, states that as early as 1100 B.C. an Egyptian temple official at Karnak, Wen-Amon, recorded an incident when a young man in Canaan, seemingly possessed by his god, behaved strangely and spoke "having his frenzy" one night.[1]

Three of Plato's dialogues refer to religious ecstatic speech. He cites the utterances of the prophetess at Delphi, the priestess at Dodona, and the Sibyl as examples of such speech. Apparently, their utterances were only considered significant when they were unintelligible. He also describes the incomprehensible speech of certain diviners whose utterances were expounded by an attendant prophet or interpreter.[2]

In the *Aeneid*, Virgil describes the sibylline priestess on the island of Delos who spoke obscurely and unintelligibly in an ecstatic state. A kind of divine inspiration supposedly caused such utterances which were considered divine oracles when interpreted by a priest or prophet.[3]

Tongues occupied a significant place in ancient Greek religion. The seeress at Delphi, not far from Corinth, spoke in tongues. According to Plutarch (A.D. 44-117), interpreters were kept in attendance to explain incoherent utterances.[4]

Others have stated that tongues were experienced in the mystery religions — Osiris, Mithra, Eleusinian, Dionysian, and Orphic cults.[5]

About A.D. 180 Celsus reported ecstatic utterances among the Gnostics. Lucian of Samosata (A.D. 120-198) described tongues-speaking as it was practiced by the devotees of the Syrian goddess, Juno.[6]

Ancient, extra-biblical occurrences of tongues verify pagan practice in this area.

Modern Occurrences

Non-Christian

Charles R. Smith points out that today witch doctors, priests and medicine men in Haiti, Greenland, Micronesia, and countries of Africa, Australia, Asia, and North and South America speak in tongues. Some use drugs to induce the utterances.[7]

Voodoo practitioners speak in tongues, as do Buddhist and Shinto priests. Moslems are also included. Their leader, Mohammed, found it difficult to return to "logical and intelligible speech" after his ecstatic experiences.[8]

V. Raymond Edman, former president of Wheaton College, reported that during their ritual dances, Tibetan monks have spoken in English, including profanity typical of drunken sailors.[9]

Tongues-speaking occurs among anti-Christian spiritist mediums.[10]

Today nonreligious tongues-speaking often occurs in association with certain mental illness. Psychiatrists have reported it in association with schizophrenia, neurosis, and psychosis. Following the extended tongues meetings held by Aimee Semple McPherson, founder of the Church of the Foursquare Gospel, mental institutions in the area of her meetings were overburdened.[11]

Tongues occurred among the worshippers of "Father Divine," who was noted both for accepting worship of himself as God and for his sexual promiscuity with his devotees.[12]

Even liberals and others who deny the inspiration of the Scriptures, the virgin birth, the deity of Christ, the substitutionary atonement, and the resurrection have become involved in tongues-speaking. Undoubtedly the vacuum created by their lack of real spiritual life has contributed much to this "replacement phenomenon" of glossolalia.

Religious Movements Before 1900

Except for the heretical Montanists, there is no clear evidence of any Christian groups practicing tongues between A.D. 55 and the seventeenth century.[13] Rogers' examination of the evidence of the church fathers in the early crucial period (A.D. 100-400) discloses that the miraculous gifts of the first century appeared to die out and were no longer needed to establish Christianity.[14]

Tongues played no part in the Reformation[15] though it is recorded that Luther dealt with the beginning of a movement.[16]

Five groups may be mentioned briefly as the only significant movements from 1600-1900 A.D.[17]

(1) **Cevenol Prophets.** Following the revocation of the Edict of Nantes in 1685, the "gift of prophecy" and ecstatic phenomena occurred among the persecuted protestants in southern France. It was said that even very young children who knew only the local dialect spoke in perfect French while in a trance. Soon the group was discredited because of their military activities and unfulfilled prophecies.

(2) The **Jansenists** were a group of Roman Catholic reformers who opposed both the Reformation and the Jesuits. They held night meetings in about 1731 at a former leader's tomb, where reportedly ecstatic phenomena, including tongues, occurred.

(3) **Shakers.** "Mother" Ann Lee founded the Shaker community near Troy, New York, in 1776. In addition to other irregularities it is said that in order to "mortify the flesh" she instituted the practice of men and women dancing together naked while they spoke in tongues.

(4) **Irvingites.** Later called the Catholic Apostolic Church, the Irvingites were founded by Edward Irving, a Scotch Presbyterian minister, who believed that all apostolic gifts should be evidenced in his day. Mary Campbell was the first of this group to speak in tongues in 1830. The group was discredited because of revelation contradictory to the Word, unfulfilled prophecies, confessions of dishonesty or satanic source by leading members, and rumors of immorality.

(5) **Mormons.** Since the beginning under Joseph Smith, the Mormons have accepted tongues as a valid gift for modern times. When their temple was dedicated in Salt Lake City, Utah, hundreds of elders spoke in tongues.

Religious Movements Since 1900

The modern charismatic Pentecostal movement may be traced back to about 1900. From the beginning of the Holiness movement in eastern Tennessee and western North Carolina in 1886, tongues and other ecstatic phenomena were common. But it was in 1901 at Bethel Bible College in Topeka, Kansas, that specific tongues activity led to the birth of Pentecostalism.[18]

Charles Parham, founder of that college and often called "the father of the modern Pentecostal movement," left town in December of 1900 for a preaching engagement after assigning his students the task of answering the question, "What is the Bible evidence of the baptism of the Holy Ghost?"

They concluded that speaking in tongues was the evidence and began to pray fervently for this experience. On January 1, 1901, student Agnes Ozman "received the baptism." Because this was the first occasion in modern times when this experience followed intense and fervent efforts to receive such a "baptism," this has been called the birthday of Pentecostalism.

A few years later, in 1905, the Azusa Street Mission was established in Los Angeles under student W.J. Seymour, and tongues appeared. This became the "Mecca" of Pentecostalism in that day with many holiness pastors flocking to this center.

Today Pentecostal churches number membership in the millions.

Until 1960 tongues-speaking, at least outwardly, was limited almost entirely to Pentecostal churches. Then on April 3, 1960, Father Dennis Bennett, rector of a large Episcopal Church in Van Nuys, California, announced to his congregation that he had spoken in tongues.[19]

This has been acclaimed as the beginning of "charismatic revival" within the historic, or "mainline" denominations. Since that date, all of the major denominations have been affected, and in recent years the greatest growth in tongues-speaking has been seen among Roman Catholics.

Conclusion

The modern tongues movement may be traced to Bethel Bible College in Topeka, Kansas, in 1901. But tongues occurred before Pentecost and have occurred since among both Christian and non-Christian groups.

Tongues entered the mainline denominations in 1960, and are now being practiced and sought by many throughout the world.

From the historical review it would appear that glossolalia is *not* an exclusively Christian demonstration, but that both Christians and non-Christians can, and in fact do, speak in tongues. However, historian George W. Dollar rightly concludes that the tongues movement "has not been, it is not, nor can it be based on church history and a stream of witness to tongues down through the centuries."[20]

CHAPTER TWO

Pentecostal Tongues
(Read Acts 2:1-21)

The charismatic movement is spreading across the world today. The movement's name comes from the Greek word *charisma* meaning gift. Abbott-Smith, in his *Manual Greek Lexicon of the New Testament*, says it is especially used "of extraordinary operations of the Spirit in the Apostolic Church."[1] Today its principal rallying point and thrust is speaking in tongues.

The Christian camp is divided on the issue. There are some who hold that the first century gift of speaking in tongues is current today. They believe the gift is evidenced by glossolalia, an expression coming from *glossa*, one of the Greek words used for tongues in the New Testament. On the other hand, others believe that the gift of tongues and some other early spiritual gifts were temporary gifts ordained by God for special purposes in the early church and are no longer current.

But most agree that some people today are speaking something they call tongues. As Dr. Charles C. Ryrie of Dallas Theological Seminary states in the forward of Joseph Dillow's book, *Speaking In Tongues*, "There is no doubt that many fine Christians are experiencing something they call tongues, and their experiences are genuine. But as with all experiences the question is not, are they genuine, but, are they scriptural?"[2]

First of all, as a background to the consideration of

pentecostal tongues in Acts 2, it is good to focus on the Lord Jesus Christ. Jesus was crucified for our sins. His resurrection proved the value of that work and the truth of His deity. For forty days "he showed Himself alive after His passion by many infallible proofs," (Acts 1:3). Then He ascended to heaven with the angelic promise of His return in like manner (v. 11).

Ten days later the waiting disciples experienced Pentecost. "And when the day of Pentecost was fully come, they were all with one accord in one place," (2:1). Pentecost was the fourth of seven great annual Jewish feasts — one of three feasts which the Jews were required to observe — the Passover Feast, the Feast of Pentecost, and the Feast of Tabernacles. The Feast of Pentecost came fifty days after Christ's resurrection and was the fulfillment of the Feast of Weeks described in Leviticus 23:15-21.

Pentecost was a feast of the harvest. The people would come to Jerusalem and assemble about the temple for the chanting of the Hallel (Ps. 113-118, each beginning with Hallelujah), and for the offering of the burnt offerings and the peace offerings. The central feature of the day was the presentation of two loaves of leavened, salted bread unto the Lord. Thanksgiving at home included a hospitable meal to which the Levite, the widow, the orphan, the poor, and the stranger were invited.[3]

But this observance of Pentecost was to be different for the one hundred and twenty gathered in the upper room. They were waiting for the "promise of the Father," (Acts 1:4), also called the baptism of the Holy Spirit (v. 5). Then it happened! The Holy Spirit came.

I. EVIDENCE OF THE SPIRIT'S COMING, vv. 1-4

Luke, the physician, describes the evidence of the Spirit's coming by the physical manifestations of the wind, the fire, and the gift of tongues.

"And suddenly there came a sound from heaven as of a rushing mighty wind and it filled all the house where they were sitting," (v. 2). Strictly speaking this was not wind. Note the word "as". A sound came from heaven, a roar or reverberation like the sound of wind which filled the house. Literally it may be translated "an echoing sound as of a mighty wind born violently."

The second evidence was fire. "And there appeared unto them cloven tongues like as of fire, and it sat upon each of them," (v. 3). The *New International Version* translates the verse as follows: "they saw what seemed to be tongues of fire that separated and came to rest upon each of them."[4]

The third evidence of the Spirit's coming was speaking in tongues. "And they were all filled with the Holy Ghost and began to speak with other tongues as the Spirit gave them utterance," (v. 4). The word tongues in Greek is *glossa* in the plural, referring to real languages which were new to the speakers. This was not jargon nor gibberish.

The Holy Spirit was the source of the enablement. "The Spirit gave them utterance," (v. 4b). Their tongues consisted of the ability to speak these languages, *not* in sensitizing the hearers' ears in some way. Note that this miracle of "Pentecostal Tongues" arose from the *filling* of the Holy Spirit, (v. 4a).

The wind, the fire, and the tongues were important to disclose and to prove to the disciples that the Holy Spirit had come into the world. This coming was in the "residential sense," remembering that God the Spirit was here all the time and exercised sovereign power in the Old Testament period, too.

But now that He had come, what is the relationship of speaking in tongues to the baptism of the Holy Spirit which Jesus had promised? This is one of the basic issues regarding pentecostal tongues.

The word baptism is not found in the immediate context and does not occur in the chapter until verse 38. However, both baptism and filling are present here.

Jesus had told his disciples that John truly baptized with water but that they would be baptized with the Holy Spirit very soon, (Acts 1:5). These two baptisms are contrasted. John's baptism was a baptism unto repentance which concerned the spiritual remnant of Israel who turned to Jehovah before Christ died, and before the church was formed by the Holy Spirit at Pentecost.

The baptism of the Holy Spirit consists of a definite union with Christ in His death and resurrection as applied to us personally. This baptism places the believer into the body of Christ, the true Church, and joins the believer to the head of that body, our Lord Jesus Christ. Two New Testament verses specifically define this baptism of the Holy Spirit. I Corinthians 12:13 states, "For by one Spirit were we all *baptized into one body*, whether we be Jews or Gentiles, whether we be bond or free; and have been all made to drink into one Spirit." Galatians 3:27 discloses, "For as many of you as have been *baptized into Christ* have put on Christ."

When Jesus spoke in Acts 1, the baptism of the Holy Spirit was still future. In Acts 11:15-16 Peter looked back to Pentecost as the historical beginning of the baptism of the Holy Spirit. "And as I began to speak," he said, "the Holy Ghost fell on them, as on us at the beginning. Then remembered I the word of the Lord that He said, John indeed baptized with water; but ye shall be baptized with the Holy Ghost."

The baptism of the Holy Spirit occurs at the moment of salvation today. Compare John 7:38-39; Rom. 8:9; I Cor. 12:13; Gal. 3:27. This is the *real* baptism relative to

Christians as contrasted to *ritual* water baptism. Once received the Spirit baptism is never repeated. It is a sovereign work of God to place me into the body of Christ. He also joins me to Christ, apart from any experience, such as speaking in tongues. God knows the moment I believe in Christ as Savior. Instantly, sovereignly, He accomplishes this glorious work of the real baptism of the Holy Spirit along with the simultaneous ministries of regeneration (John 3:1-8), sealing (Eph. 4:30), and indwelling (I Cor. 6:19).

Therefore, the baptism of the Holy Spirit concerns relationship to God in His family. Because of this relationship the believer receives power with special emphasis on witnessing. "But ye shall receive power after that the Holy Ghost is come upon you: and ye shall be witnesses unto me both in Jerusalem and all Judaea, and in Samaria, and unto the uttermost part of the earth," (Acts 1:8).

An important issue. A leading charismatic writer, Don W. Basham in his book, *A Handbook on Holy Spirit Baptism*, states, "The baptism in the Holy Spirit is a second encounter with God (the first is conversion) in which the Christian begins to receive the supernatural power of the Holy Spirit into his life . . . the Christian is brought into a deeper relationship with Christ . . ."[5]

It's true that believers need a deeper and more meaningful walk with the Lord Jesus. But for a believer to seek the baptism of the Holy Spirit is to go totally against the revealed Word of God which states that every believer is already baptized with the Holy Spirit, i.e. is placed into the body of Christ and joined to Christ.

Some charismatics, as Smith says,[6] suggest two spiritual baptisms — the baptism *by* the Holy Spirit (salvation) and the baptism *with* or *in* the Holy Spirit signified by tongues later. This cannot be supported.

Ephesians 4:5 speaks of only *one* baptism. Neither can the prepositional distinction (by, with, in) be sustained. The same Greek preposition (en) is used in both Acts 1:5 and in I Corinthians 12:13. Furthermore, the last phrase of I Cor. 12:13 is not distinct from but rather parallel to the first part of that verse.

Some say that speaking in tongues is a primary evidence or even the only evidence of the baptism of the Holy Spirit. But in I Corinthians 12:29-30 where a series of questions is asked, because of the way the Greek is phrased, a negative answer is expected to all of the questions. In verse 30 Paul says, "Do all speak with tongues?" The answer, therefore, is, "No, *not all* speak with tongues." However, I Cor. 12:13a says, "For by one Spirit are we *all* baptized into one body" (lit. "were baptized" — aorist passive). While not all believers speak in tongues, *all* believers have been baptized with the Holy Spirit. Therefore, speaking in tongues cannot be the sign of the baptism of the Holy Spirit. All Christians are baptized by the Holy Spirit, but "not all speak with tongues."

Dillow suggests seven evidences of having been baptized with the Holy Spirit. They are *not miraculous but moral, not ecstatic but ethical* — really evidences of being a born-again believer and a Christian. They are as follows:[7]

1) Praying to God as your Father, Galatians 4:6; Romans 8:15-16.
2) An understanding of the grace of God, I Corinthians 2:12.
3) A consciousness of the love of God, Romans 5:5.
4) An assurance of salvation, II Corinthians 1:22.
5) A confession of the humanity of Jesus, I John 4:2-3.
6) The fruit of the Spirit, Galatians 5:22-23. An absence of these wonderful characteristics could indicate immaturity or carnality.

7) Love for other Christians, I John 4:12-13.

What wonderful evidences of the baptism of the Holy Spirit — and all without speaking in tongues!

The baptism of the Holy Spirit is always presented as a statement of fact rather than something one is commanded to seek. If it were important for our Christian experience to seek the baptism of the Spirit *after* salvation, why is it never commanded?

Just as the wind, the fire, and the tongues gave evidence of the Spirit's coming at Pentecost, so the seven evidences above demonstrate the baptism of the Holy Spirit today.

II. EFFECTS OF THE COMING OF THE HOLY SPIRIT, vv. 5-13

In Acts 2 Jews from various lands came to Jerusalem for the Feast of Pentecost. The list in verses 9-11a reveals Jewish representatives from all over the Middle East. These foreign Jews heard the disciples speak to them in their own foreign tongues or languages. "Now when this was noised abroad, the multitude came together and were confounded because that every man heard them speak in his own language," (v. 6).

The word for language here differs from that for tongues in verse 4 (*glossa*) and confirms the presence of real languages. It is the word *dialektos* or dialect. The reaction of the Jewish visitors was understandable. "And they were all amazed and marvelled, saying one to another, Behold, are not all these which speak Galileans? And how hear we every man in our own tongue (dialect) wherein we were born?" (vv. 7-8).

The visiting Jews state in verse 11, "We do hear them speak in our tongues the wonderful works of God."

Again the word tongues is *glossa*, revealing an interchangeable use of "dialect" and "tongues" in the passage. The word for "wonderful works" is *megaleia* or "the great things" of God, suggesting the lofty content of the tongues-speaking.

The visiting Jews heard the wonderful works of God. "The tongues-speaking served only an indirect evangelistic purpose, in that the tongues phenomenon prepared the way for Peter's convicting message."[8] An authenticated, confirmed apostle then saw three thousand added to the church (v. 41).

Tongues here, as later, were for a sign to the unbelieving Jews — to some whose unbelief in Jesus changed to true faith and to others whose confirmed unbelief would lead to judgment. It is important to note that Jews were present at Pentecost when tongues were spoken.

Their reaction was progressive. They were "confounded," verse 6; they "marvelled," verse 7; they "were perplexed," verse 12; in fact, reality brought "amazement," verses 7 and 12.

Many did not understand what was going on. Since ignorance is always a blow to man's pride, some, apparently native Jews, were driven to criticism and mocked (v. 13). They concluded that the disciples were drunk.

Paul later said, "And be not drunk with wine wherein is excess; but be filled with the Spirit," (Eph. 5:18). Control is the issue, but those Jews voted for the first option, never dreaming that the second was the true reality.

The filling of the Holy Spirit precedes and is contemporary with tongues-speaking at Pentecost, but this is the only reference where that filling and tongues come together (Acts 2:4). Tongues are usually identified with the baptism of the Holy Spirit in the contemporary scene.

Some charismatics, however, hold to the sovereign, positional aspect of the Spirit's baptism, then see tongues proceeding out of the filling of the Holy Spirit rather than the baptism of the Holy Spirit.

If this is the case, the general content of these chapters will apply to tongues relating to the filling of the Holy Spirit as well as to tongues relating to the baptism of the Holy Spirit.

Dr. Lewis Sperry Chafer, founder and past president of Dallas Theological Seminary, has expressed the issue well, "The Spirit's filling is not a receiving of the Holy Spirit, since that was accomplished as a part of salvation, nor is it a receiving of more of the Spirit. He is a Person, and by a yieldedness of the believer's life to Him, the Spirit will fulfill all that He came into the heart to do. The Spirit-filled life is a realization in actual experience of what has been possessed from the moment one is saved. The command to be filled indicates that the Christian's own fellowship with the Lord and faithfulness determines the degree of filling."[9]

III. EXPLANATION OF THE COMING OF THE HOLY SPIRIT, vv. 14-21

The filling of the Holy Spirit and control by that Spirit provided the answer for the meaning of tongues at Pentecost, but some were not persuaded. Therefore, Peter dealt with the first option of drunkenness and denied it. "For these are not drunken as ye suppose, seeing it is but the third hour of the day," (Acts 2:15), i.e. 9:00 a.m.

Peter goes on to say, "But this is that which was spoken by the prophet Joel," (v. 16). Peter quotes Joel 2:28-32 and links Pentecost with Joel's prophecy. Joel's theme is the day of the Lord — a day both of judgment of the Great Tribulation and kingdom blessing following. In fact, Joel 2:21-27 tells of that kingdom blessing.

In Joel 2:28, the prophet speaks of an outpouring of the Holy Spirit in the latter days. "And it shall come to pass afterward, that I will pour out my Spirit upon all flesh . . . " Joel pinpoints the time of the Spirit's outpouring in this passage. It is "afterward" (not before), that is, after Jesus Christ has returned and Israel is established in a kingdom. The fulfillment is still to come. The context of Joel 2 does not allow us to link this outpouring of the Spirit to events before Christ returns, thus refuting the thought that present day tongues are "signs of the times" — a sign that Christ is coming back soon. The "afterward" of Joel is the "last days" of Acts 2:17, referring to the days of Israel's exaltation and blessing after Christ's return.

The reference in Joel is to the ultimate, complete fulfillment at the beginning of Messiah's earthly kingdom and reign. Nothing is said of tongues directly. When Peter said, "this is that," he was referring to a partial fulfillment which occurred at Pentecost, *not* to the ultimate and complete fulfillment.

Charismatics often use this Joel passage to support the continuance of tongues today. In Joel 2:23 the prophet cites "the former rain and the latter rain." The former rain, they say, is supposed to be the initial outpouring of the Spirit in Acts 2, and the latter rain is the present-day manifestation of the Holy Spirit. The context, however, besides speaking of literal rain, refers to the "former rain" as the riches of the Jewish kingdom under David and Solomon. The "latter rain" refers to the even greater magnitude of the Jewish kingdom under the Messiah at the second coming of Christ.[10]

Peter was explaining Pentecost by stating that it was a partial fulfillment of God's promise in Joel, only a glimmer of that which will come one day when Christ returns and Israel is blessed.

After discussing the pouring out of the Spirit, both Joel 2:30-31 and Acts 2:19-20 *then* refer to signs preceding Christ's second glorious advent to the earth.

In conclusion, the Scriptures disclose that the New Testament gift of tongues was real. It came at Pentecost and involved the Spirit enabling people to speak in real languages or dialects.

Second, the baptism of the Holy Spirit concerns the believer being placed into the body of Christ and being joined to Christ at the moment of salvation. It is not to be sought. Nor are tongues the evidence of that baptism today.

Third, part of the purpose of tongues was to evidence the Holy Spirit's coming and presence to form the New Testament Church. Tongues were to prepare the way by miraculous authentication for Peter's convicting message of salvation at that time.

Fourth, tongues' purpose also involved tongues "for a sign" to the unbelieving Jews — to some whose unbelief in Jesus changed to true faith, and to others whose confirmed unbelief would lead to judgment.

Driving along the highway one day I heard the Harvest Time Broadcast of the United Pentecostal Church say, "You'll find real living when you find your Pentecost!"[11] This promise depends on what one means by "your Pentecost" — tongues or relationship.

The Word states, "And it shall come to pass, that whosoever shall call on the name of the Lord shall be saved," (Acts 2:21). "For the promise is unto you, and to your children, and to all that are afar off, even as many as the Lord our God shall call," (Acts 2:39).

As we call on the name of the Lord as He calls us, real living can flow out of a personal relationship to Jesus Christ by faith and the subsequent dedicated walk in Him! That is "finding" our Pentecost!

Fig. 1 "SCRIPTURAL SITES OF TONGUES-SPEAKING

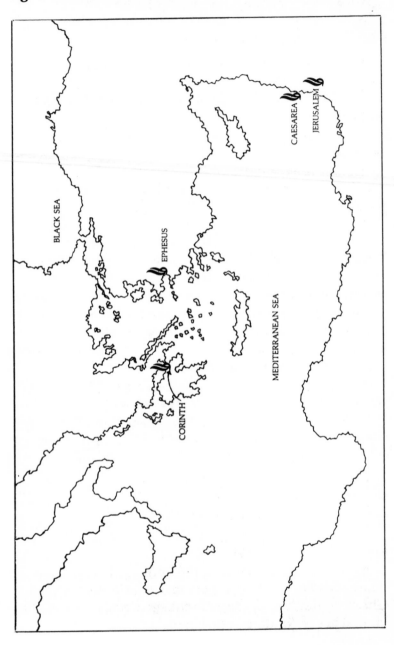

CHAPTER THREE

Speaking in Tongues at Caesarea and at Ephesus

(Read Acts 10:44-48 and Acts 19:1-7)

In the book of Acts only three situations relate directly to speaking in tongues. These are found in Acts 2, 10, and 19. The first of these references, Acts 2, was considered in the preceding chapter. Between chapters 2 and 10 all of the action occurs without reference to tongues.

In chapter 3 a lame man is healed. As Peter and others preach, the number of believers grows to about five thousand. Luke records in chapter 4 that persecution begins. However, the Christians were filled with the Holy Spirit in spite of this persecution. The filling did not result in speaking in tongues but in the preaching of the Word of God with boldness. "And when they had prayed, the place was shaken where they were assembled together; and they were all filled with the Holy Ghost, and they spake the Word of God with boldness," (4:31). Whether the Holy Spirit ministered in baptism or in filling, it is important to discern that speaking in tongues was not always the evidence of that ministry. On this occasion in Jerusalem the filling of the Holy Spirit led to power in preaching the Word.

Furthermore, there was great unity in the early church. Sin against the body was judged by immediate death, as chapter 5 indicates.

Chapters 6 through 9 speak of more persecution, the account of deacon Stephen, the first Christian martyr, and the beginning of Paul's activities and his salvation. Five to eight years probably elapsed between Acts 2 and 10 without mention of tongues.

Philip's Samaritan evangelistic tour in Acts 8 seems to give credence to Holy Spirit baptism following salvation today. Though tongues are not stated as present, Acts 8 presents a clear case of New Testament saints at Samaria who believed in Christ but did not receive the Spirit until after their salvation. There is a reason for this. One of the major problems of the transitional age from the Old Testament to the New Testament was that of convincing the Jews in Jerusalem that the blessings poured out from God were for Samaritans and Gentiles as well as for Jews. The delay of the Samaritans' receiving the Holy Spirit allowed time for Peter and John to get to Samaria and to lay hands on them for the Spirit's reception. The effect of this was the preservation of unity — the revelation to the Samaritan believers that they were of the same faith as Jerusalem believers, and the revelation to Jerusalem believers that the Samaritans could be saved.

Dr. John G. Mitchell, founder of Multnomah School of the Bible, observes in this regard, "Why is there no mention here of speaking in tongues? Because there were no unbelieving Jews present."[1] The significance of this fact will be developed more fully in chapters 9 and 11.

Now to look at the second direct reference on tongues in Acts . . .

I. SPEAKING IN TONGUES AT CAESAREA,
Acts 10:44-48

In Caesarea, a leading port on the Mediterranean Sea,

God used Peter to open the door of the gospel to the Gentiles just as he had used him earlier to open the door of the gospel to the Jews at Pentecost in Jerusalem.

Acts 10 tells of the startling vision of the Roman centurion, Cornelius, of Caesarea. He was to call for Peter to come to him. Peter, meantime, had his own vision of a great sheet let down from heaven with unclean creatures in it. The latter vision prepared Peter to witness to the Gentiles, who were unclean to Jewish minds. "Rise, Peter, kill and eat," (Acts 10:13b).

Obediently Peter traveled to Caesarea from Joppa, a near-by port city, (11:12) with six Jewish brethren, and preached the gospel to the Gentile Cornelius and to those with him. Many listeners, including Cornelius, were saved. Acts 10:34-43 recounts the incident which concludes, "to Him give all the prophets witness that through His name *whosoever* believeth in Him shall receive remission of sins."

Look closely at the concluding verses of Acts 10 to see what happened. Cornelius, his family, and friends *heard the Word*, verse 44. It is strongly implied that they *believed* that Word. Tie in Acts 10:43, quoted above, with Acts 11:17 to resource the sure fact of their faith: "forasmuch then as God gave them the like gift as He did to us who *believed* on the Lord Jesus Christ; what was I, that I could withstand God?"

A number of descriptive references to the Holy Spirit now unfold. First, in verse 44, the Word says, "the Holy Ghost *fell* on all of them." Second, the last part of verse 45 says, "on the Gentiles *also* was poured out the *gift* of the Holy Ghost." Third, in verse 47, Peter says, "can any man forbid water (ritual baptism), that these should not be baptized, which have *received the Holy Ghost* (real baptism) as well as we?"

All of this action is verified in Peter's account to the

questioning Jews at Jerusalem in Acts 11, verses 13b-18. At the time of the salvation of Cornelius, his family, and friends, they were baptized by the Holy Spirit — placed into the body of Christ and joined to the head of that body, the Lord Jesus Christ. What happened there is the normal procedure in this age of grace for all believers today — hear the gospel, believe, and be baptized by the Holy Spirit. Race or ethnic background is seen as irrelevant. Having received the *real* baptism of the Holy Spirit, they were commanded subsequently to proceed with the *ritual* baptism, water baptism. "And he commanded them to be baptized in the name of the Lord," (10:48a).

In summary note that these new Gentile believers immediately, spontaneously spoke with tongues, *glossa*, understandable, real languages.

There was a special reason why these Gentiles spoke in tongues at this point. Outward confirmation was necessary so that the six Jews who had come with Peter from Joppa could know that the Gentiles had received the Holy Spirit, were really saved, and were a part of the body of Christ and the family of God. Note the word *"for"* in verse 46, giving an evidential reason for the possession of the Holy Ghost by the Gentiles.

The word translated "magnifying" (*megalunonton*) is similar to the expression *megaleia* found in Acts 2:11, indicating that the content of the tongues-speaking was the same both in Acts 2 and in Acts 10 — praising God for His greatness and magnifying Him! This action astonished the circumcision, those Jews who had come with Peter from Joppa, verses 45-46.

Do not miss the import of the word *"also"* in verse 45. Not only Jews, but also Gentile believers received the Holy Spirit. The Jewish reaction was crystallized later in Jerusalem as Peter recalled the whole Caesarean scene in vindication of his ministry to the Gentiles. "When they heard these things they held their peace and glorified God, saying, then hath God *also* to the Gentiles granted repentance unto life," (11:18).

Thus we have a transition passage from the Old Testament order to the New Testament order, and speaking in tongues gave proof of that transition — that both Jews and Gentiles could receive the Holy Spirit with no other condition than simple faith in the Lord Jesus Christ.

Tongues were a sign to these *Jews* who, though they themselves believed, *did not believe* that Gentiles could be saved. John G. Mitchell again asks, "Why did Cornelius speak in tongues? Because there were *Christian Jews present who did not believe* (italics mine) that the Spirit of God was for Gentiles."[2]

II. SPEAKING IN TONGUES AT EPHESUS,
Acts 19:1-7

Between chapters 10 and 19 of Acts occurs a lapse of about 13 years (A.D. 41-A.D. 54). The interval is filled with the account of many cities and sermons as a part of the Apostle Paul's two missionary journeys. Throughout this extended period of time with its many movings of the Spirit, nothing is recorded of speaking in tongues until near the beginning of Paul's third missionary journey in Acts 19. Here Paul enters the tongues picture with a small group at Ephesus.

"And it came to pass, that, while Apollos was at Corinth, Paul having passed through the upper coast, came to Ephesus: and finding certain disciples, he said unto them, have ye received the Holy Ghost since ye believed? And they said unto him, we have not so much as heard whether there be any Holy Ghost," (Acts 19:1-2).

The mistranslation of verse 2 in the King James

Version has contributed much to the wrong meaning of when and how the Holy Spirit is received today.

The verse seems to say, "have you received the Holy Spirit *since* ye believed?" as if the baptism of the Holy Spirit follows the conversion experience. This is what charismatics are strongly affirming today — that the Holy Spirit baptism is something to seek in order to have a fuller and deeper life after being saved. "Seek the baptism of the Holy Spirit and its evidence in tongues!"

However, the correct translation of the first part of verse 2 is, "did ye receive the Holy Spirit *when* ye believed?" If the Ephesians had believed in Jesus Christ as their personal Savior, they should have already received the Holy Spirit. But listen to their answer. "And they said unto him (Paul), we have not so much as heard whether there be any Holy Ghost," (v. 2b).

Paul promptly administered the "baptism check" (vv. 3-4). "And he said unto them, unto what then were ye baptized? And they said, unto John's baptism. Then said Paul, John verily baptized with the baptism of repentance, saying unto the people, that they should believe on Him which should come after him, that is, on Christ Jesus," (vv. 3-4). The Ephesians knew only the baptism of John which Apollos had brought to them (Acts 18:24ff). They knew nothing at this moment of the baptism of the Holy Spirit. Paul's check proved this.

Illumination from Paul brought faith in Christ, and they were baptized with water. Verse 5 contains the only instance of rebaptism with water in the New Testament. These twelve Ephesian men believed and were baptized with water, but something more wonderful happened to them. They were brought into the body of Christ. "And when Paul had laid his hands upon them, the Holy Ghost came on them; and they spake with tongues, and prophesied," (v. 6).

A short but logical delay of the baptism of the Holy Spirit is evident here as in Acts 8 and for the same reason. Paul's laying on of hands identified this small group of Ephesians with the great Christian movement. It was similar to the salvation of the new Samaritan believers through Peter, John, and deacon Philip in Acts 8, though in Acts 8 no reference is made to the new believers speaking in tongues.

Speaking in tongues added evidence that these Ephesians were brought into the body of Christ. Again the word used is *glossa,* intelligible languages. As at Caesarea, tongues were a sign to "unbelieving" Jews, through "believing" Paul, that Gentiles also could be saved and be a part of the body of Christ. Unbelieving Jews were present at Ephesus (Acts 18:26; 19:8-9).

Here is another transition. Acts is a transitional book, spanning the years between the synagogue and the church, from law to grace, from the Old Testament saints to the New Testament Christians, from an essentially Jewish body of believers to the body of Christ in which there is neither Jew nor Gentile.[3]

Remember that Acts 2, in part, marked the outpouring of the Holy Spirit on Old Testament saints, such as the disciples. These were already converted, having heard and having believed the promises of God concerning the Messiah, Jesus. They were justified by their faith in Him and immediately placed in the body of Christ, the true church. Once, however, the transition between the old and the new covenants had been accomplished, with the Spirit poured out, He was then available to all who believed in Christ at the very point in time when they believed. This is the pattern of God's working today.

Peter was present in Acts 2, Acts 8, and in Acts 10. There must be *one* Church . . . not a Jewish Church, a Samaritan Church, and a Gentile Church. Jewish witnesses verified the validity of the experiences of these other groups and thus their speaking in tongues was God's appointed plan at that time.

In conclusion, the graphic experience of speaking in tongues at Caesarea ånd at Ephesus was to prove to the Jewish Christians that these Gentile Christians were of the same body, the body of Christ, His true church.

There was need for speaking in tongues. God wanted to make it very clear who belonged! This, however, was a transitional stage. Once the clarification was demonstrated by speaking in tongues, there was no further need of speaking in tongues to evidence entrance into the body of Christ.

Furthermore, observe that the sign gift of speaking in tongues was operative in Acts 2 (Pentecost), Acts 10 (Caesarea), and Acts 19 (Ephesus), where Jews were present. But the Word does not state tongues were spoken in Acts 8 (Samaria) where unbelieving Jews were not present.

CHAPTER FOUR

A Look at
the Corinthian Church

(Read I Corinthians 1:10-17 and I Corinthians 3:1-8)

Should a Christian seek to speak in tongues today? Should he follow the example of one minister who was reported spending twenty minutes a day seeking to achieve this experience, presumably for a deeper spiritual walk? Why or why not?

Besides the book of Acts, one other major passage concerns tongues in the New Testament — I Corinthians 12-14. From that principal passage many issues arise, but first a look at the Corinthian Church is important as a setting for these issues.

Unfortunately, this has been a long-neglected area in considering the modern tongues movement. Merely to say "Corinth was Paul's problem church" does not provide the proper impact. Before studying I Corinthians 12-14, therefore, one must look at the background of Corinth and the local church there.

I. CITY AND DESCRIPTION

Location. Corinth was located in southern Greece upon an isthmus between the gulfs of Lepanto and Aegina connecting the Peloponnesus and the mainland, forty miles west of Athens.

It had two harbors (some say three), Cenchreae on the east and Lechaeum on the west, thus commanding traffic on both the western and eastern seas.[1] A ship canal joins these harbors now. Corinth provided the link between the east and the west and also between the north and the south due to its connection of the mainland with the Peloponnesus. Its citadel, called Acrocorinthus, was built upon the rock two thousand feet above the sea.

History. Archeological discoveries have uncovered much of Paul's city. In fact, the American School of Classical Studies has excavated Corinth for thirty years.[2] There is a modern Corinth, but only a village called Gortho exists amongst the ancient ruins.

Phoenicians settled in Corinth very early, leaving traces of their civilization in art such as dyeing and weaving, as well as in religion and mythology.[3] The Corinthian cults of Aphrodite and of Athene Phoenike, both of Phoenician origin, existed there, so heathen deities were prominent.[4]

The goddess Aphrodite was the Greek name for the god whom the Romans worshipped as Venus, the goddess of lust or carnal love. In celebrating the rites of Aphrodite the Corinthians gave themselves up to the most shameful licentiousness.[5]

So notorious was the Corinthian immorality that in all parts of the Greek-speaking world, if men or women were found behaving in an unclean way, the worst anyone could say of them was that they acted like Corinthians. Corinth was the city of vice unsurpassed in the Roman world.

Corinth was the capitol of the province of Achaia, a leading Greek city of some six hundred to seven hundred thousand people in Paul's day.[6] Its population was mixed — Roman, Greek and Jewish.[7]

It was noted for its arts and architecture, for its commercial and materialistic spirit. Someone has said,

"Corinth was a city of commerce, culture, religion, and vice — a city which portrays in miniature the civilization of which we are a part today."[8] The Isthmian games were held ten miles outside the city every four years.[9]

Corinth was destroyed by the Romans in 146 B.C., then rebuilt by Julius Caesar in 46 B.C.[10] Paul arrived about one hundred years later.

It was wealthy, cosmopolitan, immoral. We are reminded in part of that wealth as Paul speaks of the gold, silver, and precious stones in chapter 3 of his first letter.

II. THE CHURCH AND ITS FORMATION

The Church at Corinth was born by the ministry of the Holy Spirit through the Apostle Paul, Silas, and Timothy on the second missionary journey, (Acts 18:1,5).

As the church grew in the great metropolis, many Jews were flocking to this center of trade. Aquila and Priscilla, tentmakers, were among these Jews. Verse 2 of Acts 18 says, "And (Paul) found a certain Jew named Aquila, born in Pontus, late come from Italy with his wife Priscilla; (because that Claudius had commanded all Jews to depart from Rome)."

Acts 18:5,8a mentions others. "And when Silas and Timotheus were come from Macedonia, Paul was pressed in the spirit, and testified to the Jews that Jesus was Christ . . . and Crispus, the chief ruler of the synagogue, believed on the Lord with all his house . . ."

The presence of these Jews provides a very important point with regard to the purpose of tongues-speaking at Corinth.

Here Paul stayed about two years preaching, teaching, and organizing the church. Because many Jews turned away in blasphemy and unbelief, Paul turned to the

Gentiles. "And when they opposed themselves, and blasphemed, he shook his raiment, and said unto them, your blood be upon your own heads; I am clean: from henceforth I will go unto the Gentiles," (Acts 18:6).

The church at Corinth represented a cross section of the citizens of the city, including male and female, Jew and Gentile, slaves and masters. However, because of Jewish unbelief the church at Corinth consisted principally of non-Jews. Justus was included, verse 7, and "many of the Corinthians hearing believed, and were baptized," (v. 8). The Lord told Paul, "I have much people in this city," (v. 10).

Acts 20 tells of Paul's continued concern for the believers as he returned to Corinth on his third missionary journey. "He came into Greece and there abode three months," (vv. 2b-3a). Paul wrote I Corinthians in A.D. 59, at the close of his three years' residence in Ephesus.

From a glimpse of the city of Corinth and the formation of the church there now turn to examine that church.

III. CHURCH EXAMINED

The Scriptures disclose the Corinthian church's wonderful position in Christ Jesus. This was a true local assembly: "unto the church of God which is at Corinth," (1:2). It was "sanctified" or set apart in Christ Jesus. They were indeed Christians and were "called saints," (v. 2).

Verse 5 discloses that they were "enriched by Him (Christ) *in all utterance.*" This relates to outward expression. Compare II Corinthians 8:7, "therefore as ye abound in everything, in faith, *and in utterance,* and knowledge, and in all diligence, and in your love to us, see that ye abound in this grace also." This may be a veiled reference to tongues. They were also enriched "in all knowledge," verse 5, which relates to inward conviction.

Verse 7 indicates the Corinthians were "waiting for the coming of our Lord Jesus Christ." They had a wonderful position in Christ. They had received much! "The grace of God was *given* them by Jesus Christ," (v. 4). And "they came behind in no *gift*," (1:7). Yet, all was not spiritually rosy in the Corinthian Church.

Specific problems existed. The Corinthian Church was not a spiritual church. In fact, of all the churches, Corinth was Paul's problem church.

Other cities had suffered a notorious background, too. Compare Ephesus and the sins surrounding the goddess Diana there. Though the Lord in Revelation 2 eventually spoke of the Ephesians losing their first love, the spiritual level of the Christians there was far higher than that of the church at Corinth. Paul's Ephesian epistle contains the highest church truth of his letters. Only a truly spiritual church could receive this. Though background is important in a church's life as well as in an individual's life and may reflect on the future, the continuing work of Christ in the heart from the moment of salvation is what really counts for effective testimony and glory to God. Unfortunately, the *Church of Corinth was not a spiritual Church.*

Division. A major symptom of their spiritual immaturity was division. "Now I beseech you, by the name of our Lord Jesus Christ, that ye all speak the same thing, and that there be no divisions among you; but that ye be perfectly joined together in the same mind and in the same judgment," (1:10). Paul voiced this appeal because of divisions in the church. Compare I Corinthians 11:18-19. "For first of all, when ye come together in the church, I hear that there be divisions among you; I partly believe it for there must be also heresies among you, that they which are approved may be made manifest among you."

There were contentions among them. "For it hath been declared unto me of you, my brethren, by them which are of the house of Chloe, that there are contentions among you," (v.11). The word for contention in the Greek, *eris*, means "strife, rangling, contention." It is used again in chapter 3, verse 3, and is translated "strife."

Paul's concern for this divisive unspiritual condition continued in his second epistle. "For I fear, lest, when I come, I will not find you such as I would, and that I shall be found unto you such as ye would not: lest there be debates, envyings, wraths, strifes, backbitings, whisperings, swellings, tumults: and lest, when I come again, my God will humble me among you, and that I shall bewail many which have sinned already and have not repented of the uncleanness and fornication and lasciviousness which they have committed," (II Cor. 12:20-21).

This spirit of division found its focal point in following human leaders. "Now this I say, that everyone of you saith, I am of Paul; and I of Apollos; and I of Cephus (Peter); and I of Christ," (I Cor. 1:12ff). The Corinthians were badly split over personalities. Have we ever heard of that in churches? A church is ruined when the people in it take their eyes off the Lord Jesus Christ and look to men.

When Clement of Rome wrote a letter to the Corinthian Church in 97 A.D., thirty-eight years later, he was dealing with the same problem—division. This is immaturity![11]

Paul makes sure that the Corinthians understood the link between childishness and division by placing the two side by side in I Corinthians 3:1-9. The first four verses read, "And I, brethren, could not speak unto you as unto spiritual, but as unto carnal, even as unto babes in Christ. I have fed you with milk, and not with meat: for hitherto ye were not able to bear it, neither yet now are ye able. For ye are yet carnal: for whereas there is among you envying, and strife, and divisions, are ye not carnal, and walk as men? For while one saith, I am of Paul; and another, I am of Apollos; are ye not carnal?" If you see divisions, you know there is carnality, fleshiness.

There is a time and place for division. In I Corinthians 10:20-21, the church is commanded not to have fellowship with those who worship devils or demons. In II Corinthians 6:14-17 the believers are commanded to avoid unrighteousness, darkness, impurity, idols, and the unclean. But as Gardiner points out "there is not a line about separating from fellow believers over personalities."[12] Such division is Corinthian immaturity!

It is important to note that today wherever speaking in tongues enters an assembly not already so oriented, strong division will enter there. The issue is likely to split the church.

Dillow states a little known fact: "An outbreak of charismatic manifestations almost destroyed the impact of the Reformation, and caused Luther to speak out against such things."[13]

Division may not be over personalities in the church today, but it can be over whether or not to speak in tongues.

Why do people choose a path that puts the unity of the body second and bypasses the headship of that body, our Lord Jesus Christ—all to emphasize the lesser gift, speaking in tongues? That gift is last in the ordered rank of spiritual gifts in I Corinthians 12:28, but it has become first in many places.

May we not conclude that whatever divides the brethren is not of the Holy Spirit (assuming, of course, that the brethren are desirous of the will of God).

Observe that the only tongues-speaking church about which one reads in the epistles was a carnal, divided church.

Paul had the answer for this problem of division. The answer was not water baptism, though the Corinthians apparently followed the leader who had baptized them. "For Christ sent me not to baptize, but to preach the Gospel," (1:17). The answer rests in preaching the gospel. Preach the cross of Christ. Put Him first and why He came and what He can do for sinners and for saints.

In I Corinthians 3 Paul emphasizes the unity of the body of Christ. This is vital. He that planted (Paul) and he that watered (Apollos) are one, but God is the One who gives the increase!

Paul's answer in part was the gospel and the unity of the body under God who alone is worthy of glory!

A look at the background of the city of Corinth and of the Corinthian Church in its formation helps us to understand its unspiritual condition and the first major symptom of spiritual immaturity which is division. The following chapter unfolds more symptoms of spiritual immaturity.

CHAPTER FIVE

Beware Corinthianism

Isn't it strange that a church so enriched by Jesus Christ, "so that (it) came behind in no gift" should be such a problem!

But the church at Corinth was a problem! A great problem to Paul and to the Lord! It was a *gifted* church. In fact, the Corinthian Church might be called a charismatic church. The Greek word for gift in verse 7 of chapter 1 is *charisma*. But it was not a spiritual church!

Their division, as noted in the preceding chapter, was a symptom of their spiritual immaturity. The Corinthians were split over personalities. Paul linked their "envying and strife, and divisions" in chapter 3 with the childishness of their spiritual immaturity.

Now note more symptoms of the Corinthian church's spiritual immaturity.

Selfishness. The people at the Corinthian Church, though "brethren" (Christians), were not spiritual but carnal, fleshly as little babies. "And I, brethren, could not speak unto you as unto spiritual, but as unto carnal, even as unto babes in Christ," (3:1).

What is one of the basic characteristics of babies? Selfishness! Some of their first words are "me, my, and mine." This is also true of babes in Christ of any age.

Paul said to the Corinthians, "I have fed you with milk and not with meat: for hitherto ye were not able to bear it, neither yet now are ye able." Spiritual babies as well as physical babies need a milk diet. They are not mature enough to eat meat.

The writer to the Hebrews accents this same thought. "For when for the time ye ought to be teachers, ye have need that one teach you again which be the first principles of the oracles of God; and are become such as have need of milk, and not of strong meat. For everyone that useth milk is unskillful in the word of righteousness: for he is a babe. But strong meat belongeth to them that are of full age, even those who by reason of use have their senses exercised to discern both good and evil," (Heb. 5:12-14).

Selfishness was manifested by the spirit of "I want my own ideas of life rather than those of God." In both chapters 2 and 3, one of the Corinthian Church's problems was human wisdom. They valued their approach to life and even looked at spiritual things from a human viewpoint. This was a form of selfish self-deception. "Let no man deceive himself. If any man among you seemeth to be wise in this world, let him become a fool, that he may be wise. For the wisdom of this world is foolishness with God. For it is written, he taketh the wise in their own craftiness. And again, the Lord knoweth the thoughts of the wise, that they are vain," (3:18-21).

Chapter 6 reveals that the Corinthians were suing each other in the courts because they felt they were being "defrauded," (vv. 6-8). They displayed selfishness with no thought of what that self-centered action would do to others.

They also selfishly misused their Christian liberties. "But take heed lest by any means this liberty of yours become a stumbling block to them that are weak. For if any man see thee which hath knowledge sit at meat in the idol's temple, shall not the conscience of him which is weak be emboldened to eat those things which are offered to idols; and through thy knowledge shall the weak brother perish, for whom Christ died?" (8:9-11).

Paul rebukes the church for selfishness at the love-feast, the agape, preceding the Lord's Supper. "When ye come together therefore into one place, this is not to eat the Lord's Supper. For in eating everyone taketh before other his own supper and one is hungry and another is drunken. What? Have ye not houses to eat and to drink in? Or despise ye the church of God and shame them that have not? What shall I say to you? Shall I praise you in this? I praise you not," (11:20-22). They were gorging themselves with food at the love-feast while the poorer saints went hungry. They were making themselves drunk with no thought of the effects. This is pure selfishness.

Would you like to look for leadership from the judgment and attitudes of the Corinthian Church.

The Corinthians were not ignorant about the gifts. They had them all, but they were wilfully ignorant concerning the proper reasons for those gifts as well as the proper use of them.

As George E. Gardiner, former charismatic, says, "The Corinthians were using the gifts for self-edification, a practice to which Paul objected in chapters twelve through fourteen."[1] Self-edification strikes at the heart of one of the strong reasons for practicing tongues-speaking today.

Beware of Corinthian selfishness. Look to the Savior and the giving of Himself in love and care for us! May that character be seen in our lives as a part of our maturity in Christ!

Besides division and selfishness, another symptom of spiritual immaturity appears.

Criticism. The Corinthian crowd "looked down their noses" at Paul because they thought they had outgrown him and had spiritually outdistanced him.

Paul said, "But with me it is a very small thing that I should be judged of you, or of man's judgment: yea, I judge not mine own self," (4:3). Their immature attitude was flashed back in a critical quotation from them which Paul uses. "For his letters, say they, are weighty and powerful but his bodily presence is weak, and his speech contemptible," (II Corinthians 10:10).

The Corinthians were Paul's spiritual children, yet they were challenging his apostleship. He was embarrassed, but he was constrained to defend his apostleship with so-called "forced boasting" in II Corinthians 11 and 12. What he was really doing was challenging their spiritual immaturity which demonstrated itself in unjustified criticism of him. Criticism has its roots in pride, and Paul put his finger on this.

"Puffed up" were Paul's words for that pride. He related their pride to their schismatic divisional spirit, too, because their criticism of him was involved in these party choices.

"And these things, brethren, I have in a figure transferred to myself and to Apollos for your sake; that ye might learn in us not to think of men above that which is written, that no one of you be puffed up for one against another," (I Cor. 4:6). Then again he said, "Now some are puffed up, as though I would not come to you. But I will come to you shortly, if the Lord will, and will know, not the speech of them that are puffed up, but the power. For the kingdom of God is not in word, but in power," (4:18-20). What counted was not the "puff" but the "power".

Through the years I have been aware of either veiled or sometimes open criticism of those who did not speak in tongues by those who did speak in tongues. The assumption was, "because I speak in tongues, I am more spiritual than you!" Where is the spirit of humility? Because of other factors tongues speakers may be "more spiritual" than those who do not speak in tongues, but tongues-speaking is not the deciding factor.

"For who maketh thee to differ from another? And what hast thou that thou didst not receive? Now if thou didst receive it, why dost thou glory, as if thou hadst not received it?" (4:7). "But the manifestation of the Spirit is given to every man to profit withal . . . but all these worketh that one and selfsame Spirit, dividing to every man severally as he will," (12:7, 11).

If the Corinthians had the gift of tongues, for example, was it to their great credit that they possessed this gift? Rather because of God's sovereign bestowal, a spirit of humility and praise would be more in order! Viewing a brother who did not possess this gift and therefore was inferior and not as spiritual in some eyes provided no cause to glory.

Satirically Paul states this same thought in the eighth verse of chapter 4, "Now ye are full, now ye are rich, ye have reigned as kings without us: and I would to God ye did reign, that we also might reign with you."

During the French and English wars, Admiral Phipps was in charge of the British fleet anchored outside of Quebec, waiting the coming of the British land forces. His orders were to remain there quietly and proceed against the city later in a planned "joint attack". Arriving early, Phipps, being an ardent non-conformist, was irritated by the statues of saints which decorated the roof and tower of the Catholic cathedral near the shore. So he spent his time shooting at them with his ships' guns. How many statues he actually hit and destroyed no one knows; but history records that when the infantry arrived, and the signal for the real attack was given, Admiral Phipps found himself out of powder and shells. He was powerless against the enemy, because he had used up his ammunition in "shooting at the saints!" Christians must beware of making the same mistake! Beware Corinthian criticism. Exercise prayer and love and self-judgment in balance, yet holding carefully to the truth.

Toleration of evil in the church was another symptom of immaturity. Jesus said the church was to be "salt" and "light" in the world, (Matt. 5:13-14). Salt holds decay in check. Light dispells darkness. The Corinthian Church was to be salt and light, and so are we.

The church at Corinth, instead of holding evil in check, was overcome by it. Far from giving light, they merged into the shadows. As one has said, "Corinth made its mark upon the church. God intended the church to make its mark upon the city!"[2] How about us? Are we really salt and light? Sadly, the Corinthian Christians tolerated evil in the church. Paul is shocked to learn of a member living immorally with his step-mother, an action even most amoral pagans frowned upon. "It is reported commonly that there is fornication among you, and such fornication as is not so much as named among the Gentiles, that one should have his father's wife and ye are puffed up, and have not rather mourned, that he that hath done this deed might be taken away from among you," (5:1-2).

They failed to realize the activity of sin in the body. Their sensitivity to sin had been dulled. They were not actually reveling over their sin but they were so puffed up in their division that they had no time to deal with the sin! They failed to mourn over sin. "Know ye not that a little leaven leaveneth the whole lump?" (5:6b).

The Corinthians failed in separation from evil. "Purge out therefore the old leaven that ye may be a new lump as ye are unleavened, for even Christ our passover is sacrificed for us," (5:7). Strong words conclude chapter 5. "But now I have written unto you not to keep company, if any man that is called a brother be a fornicator, or covetous, or an idolater, or a railer, or a drunkard, or an extortioner; with such an one no not to eat. For what have I to do to judge them also that are without? Do not ye judge them that are within? But them that are without God judgeth. Therefore, put away from among yourselves that wicked person," (5:11-13).

Some Corinthian Christians were involved with prostitutes, perhaps identifying with the pagan temple worship all around them. "Know ye not that your bodies are the members of Christ? Shall I then take the members of Christ, and make them the members of an harlot? God forbid. What? Know ye not that he which is joined to an harlot is one body? For two, saith he, shall be one flesh. For he that is joined unto the Lord is one spirit. Flee fornication. Every sin that a man doeth is without the body; but he that committeth fornication sinneth against his own body," (6:15-18).

They had to be reminded that their bodies were the temple of the Holy Spirit. "What? Know ye not that your body is the temple of the Holy Ghost which is in you, which ye have of God, and ye are not your own? For ye are bought with a price; therefore glorify God in your body, and in your spirit, which are God's," (6:19-20).

Heresy in the Church. Part of this evil which was being tolerated by the Corinthians was moral; part was doctrinal, i.e. heresy was infiltrating the church. Heresy usually accompanies the presence of evil in a church. "Know ye not that ye are the temple of God, and that the Spirit of God dwelleth in you? If any man defile the temple of God, him shall God destroy; for the temple of God is holy, which temple ye are," (3:16-17). God's temple had been defiled. The reference later is to the physical temple of the body. Here the thought concerns the spiritual temple of the church which was being defiled by false teachers.

Even the doctrine of the resurrection was being questioned by some in the congregation. "Now if Christ be preached that he rose from the dead, how say some among you that there is no resurrection of the dead?" (15:12).

Again Paul states, "But I fear, lest by any means, as the serpent beguiled Eve through his subtility, so your minds should be corrupted from the simplicity that is in

Christ," (II Cor. 11:3). Later he commands them to "examine yourselves, whether ye be in the faith," (II Cor. 13:5).

Here was a church which was arrested in development, charismatic in practice, immoral in living, and heretical in part in doctrine. Paul wrote with a broken heart to a church over which he had expended so much time and effort and teaching—a tragedy. Beware of Corinthian toleration of evil. Beware Corinthianism!

Great Principle! Spiritual maturity is not determined by the possession nor the exercise of spiritual gifts.

Dr. Charles Ryrie defines spiritual maturity together with its formula, saying, "Spiritual maturity is the growth which the Holy Spirit produces over a period of time in the believer."[3]

The formula: $R \times T = D$. R stands for the rate of growth. T depicts time and D stands for maturity. In other words, rate of growth multiplied by time equals maturity. The goal is Christian maturity. It will take more or less time to accomplish this. Therefore, the key factor is the rate of growth, or the work of the Holy Spirit in the life.

Some charismatics state that tongues determine this R factor, this rate of growth for spiritual maturity. The Word of God does not support such a claim, and the example of the Corinthians disproves that claim.

The careful reading of the Word of God, prayer, and obedience to the Word of God which results in worship, fellowship, and witnessing will contribute to the demonstration of the fruit of the Spirit in the believer's life, as one yields himself to His control. Therefore, the believer does not need to seek a gift of tongues for spiritual maturity.

Division, selfishness, criticism, and toleration of evil, both personal and doctrinal, highlighted the spiritual immaturity of the Corinthian Church. Instead of these symptoms, the Holy Spirit desired to produce His fruit!

CHAPTER SIX

Charismatic Source and Diversity

(Read I Corinthians 12:1-11)

We have looked at the book of Acts, and we have also considered the long-neglected theme of the Corinthian Church. The Corinthian Church was a most gifted Church, but unfortunately, it was not a spiritual church even though more is said about its relation to tongues than any other church.

It is apparent that spiritual maturity is not determined by the possession of nor the exercise of spiritual gifts. Instead, maturity is determined by the growth produced in the believer by the Holy Spirit of God as that believer yields to Him through continued exposure to the Word of God, prayer, obedience, and witnessing.

Focus now on the second major passage in the New Testament on tongues, I Corinthians 12-14. Here the word "tongue(s)" is used twenty-one times: chapter 12, 4 times; chapter 13, 2 times; chapter 14, 15 times. The significant thing about these occurrences is that the same Greek word used in Acts, *glossa*, appears throughout here.

The italicized word *unknown* in chapter 14 (used six times) is not in the original but has been supplied by the translators and should be omitted.

Real languages occur in the book of Acts. Since the word *glossa* is the same in I Corinthians as in Acts, remembering the omission of the italicized word *unknown*, there is evidence that the gift of tongues is real languages here also.

Some have claimed that the Corinthian tongues were ecstatic utterances, at least in part, in contrast to the real languages of Acts, but this cannot be substantiated by the text. Any ecstatic gibberish could be traced to heathen origin. Zeller lists twelve reasons why Biblical tongues were real languages. These may be condensed as follows:[1]

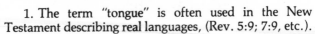

1. The term "tongue" is often used in the New Testament describing real languages, (Rev. 5:9; 7:9, etc.).

2. The adjective "new" is most appropriate for describing real languages (Mark 16:17)—totally new to the speaker as a foreign language.

3. Speaking in tongues was a supernatural, God-given ability (Mark 16:17-18; Acts 2:4), reasonable only if tongues were real languages.

4. The adjective "other" is very appropriate for describing real languages (Acts 2:4; I Cor. 14:21; cf. Isaiah 28:11).

5. The tongues of Acts 2:4, 11 are clearly identified in Acts 2:6, 8 as real languages (dialects).

6. The tongues of both Acts (2:11; 10:46) and I Corinthians (14:14-15—prayer; 14:15—praise; 14:16—giving of thanks) conveyed a message with either doctrinal or meaningful content, not empty gibberish.

7. The expression "kinds of tongues" is understandable only if tongues were real languages, (I Cor. 12:10, 28; 14:10).

8. The fact that tongues could be interpreted demands that tongues be real languages, (I Cor. 12:10, 30; 14:5, 13, 27-28). Interpretation necessitates meaning.

9. I Corinthians 14:10-11 clearly depicts real languages.

10. Tongues-speaking is said to consist of *words*, only possible if tongues were real languages, (I Cor. 14:9, 19).

11. The tongues of Isaiah 28:11 quoted by Paul in I Corinthians 14:21 were real languages.

12. The article of previous reference in I Corinthians 14:22 proves that the Corinthian tongues (v. 22) were the very same thing as the Isaiah tongues (v. 21), namely, real languages.

This section of Paul's first epistle to the Corinthian Church may be summarized as follows: chapter 12 gives the *principles* of the gifts; chapter 13 *guards* against making these gifts the supreme object of life, which supremacy belongs to our Lord Jesus Christ; and chapter 14 tells us of the *exercise* of these gifts.

I. THE GREAT TEST OF UTTERANCE IN THE SPIRIT, vv. 1-3

First of all, Paul presents principles of the gifts to dislodge ignorance and misunderstanding.

"Now concerning spiritual gifts, brethren, I would not have you ignorant," (12:1). The word *gifts* is not in the original. Before us we have the *pneumatika* or the "spirituals". These are "things which pertain to the Holy Spirit." This word is used again in chapter 14, verse 1, and comes from the same root word as that for the Holy Spirit *(pneuma)*. It may suggest essence (intrinsic nature)[2] in contrast to the gifts themselves (v. 4, etc.).

The emphasis is on two things: first of all, the essence or intrinsic nature of the gifts which is spiritual and, secondly, the source of the gifts which is the Holy Spirit. Paul does not want the Corinthian Church to be ignorant of these things, nor does the Lord want us to be ignorant of them. Apparently, though the Corinthians possessed the gifts, they were ignorant of both the purpose and the use of these gifts.

In verse two Paul reminds them of their past, unconverted state. "Ye know that ye were Gentiles, carried away unto these dumb idols, even as ye were led." "Carried away" or "led away" has the force of being "swept away" *(apago)*. What an interesting statement! Before becoming Christians they had placed great importance on being swept away in a demonstration of ecstacy, a part of the Greek mystery religions.

Plato and Virgil tell of such devotees caught up in emotional hysteria, shaking and falling prostrate on the ground and babbling in ecstatic speech.[3] Paul is saying, "that is the way it was when you were idolaters, but it should not be so now!"

Charles R. Smith speaks of pre-Christian tongues and of non-Christian tongues.[4] Apparently, the Corinthians were still placing importance on this "being-swept-away" phenomenon and Paul begins to correct them. "This is not a sign of spirituality," he is saying, "but of your heathen days."

In the charismatic movement today there is an over-emphasis for some on "being carried away" or "being slain in the spirit". This kind of expressive display or experience has no part in the New Testament record.[5]

Dillow states that "it is paralleled all over the world as a common occult phenomenon! But the ecstacy of the experience is mistaken for the presence of the Holy Spirit."[6] However, the Holy Spirit does not produce what idolatrous worship produces!

Great test, v. 3. "Wherefore I give you to understand, that no man speaking by the Spirit of God calleth Jesus accursed: and no man can say that Jesus is the Lord, but by the Holy Ghost." Do you call "Jesus accursed" or "Jesus Lord"? These appear as titles in the Greek. The one title was the cry of the pagans in hatred, the other the cry of the Christians in faith. Here was a line of demarcation between people, and the possession of the Holy Spirit made the difference.[7]

This was a criteria whereby one might test the utterance of a speaker in an assembly. We have the test of the Word of God today, but they did not have that test then.

The real test of a spiritual gift is whether or not it promotes the glory of God, the lordship of Jesus Christ, and edifies His church. The issue is not just the repetition of a phrase. You could get someone on the street to do this for a few dollars. The issue is belief in the sovereignty of Christ.

Jesus said that the Holy Spirit would not speak of Himself nor promote Himself but would always speak of and promote the Lord Jesus Christ. "Howbeit when He the Spirit of truth is come, He will guide you into all truth: for He shall not speak of Himself; but whatsoever He shall hear, that shall He speak: and He will show you things to come. He shall glorify Me: for He shall receive of mine and shall show it unto you," (John 16:13-14). The Spirit of truth shall not speak of nor from Himself. His purpose is to glorify Christ and to receive the things of Christ and show them unto us.

The Holy Spirit is God the third person, equal in power, attributes and authority to God the Father and God the Son. But His special ministry is to always exalt Christ. In determining if any movement is of God, a basic criteria will be the exaltation of Jesus Christ. That is the heart of I Corinthians 12:3.

The Holy Spirit will never lower the value of Christ nor His work. Dr. Earl D. Radmacher, president of Western Conservative Baptist Seminary, rightly concludes, "Any man who is truly honoring Jesus Christ will never espouse a doctrine that will in any way depreciate Jesus Christ. No doctrine is of the Holy Spirit which depreciates Jesus Christ."[8]

For example, the Holy Spirit never is the author of such a statement as this: "now that you have received Christ you have salvation, but you need to receive the Holy Spirit to be a complete Christian."[9] Behind such a statement is the idea that Christ begins the work of salvation, but that the Holy Spirit completes it. This is not true scripturally. "And He is the head of the body, the church: who is the beginning, the firstborn from the dead; that in all things He might have the preeminence. For it pleased the Father that in Him should all fulness dwell," (Col. 1:18-19). In all the facets of the Holy Spirit's work, particularly with reference to the believer, He is committed to the preeminence of Jesus Christ!

Gardiner summarizes these first three verses with four vital principles:[10]

1. God intends His people to be concerned with the total of the spiritual life, not just the spiritual gifts.

2. God does not want us to be ignorant of the purpose of His gifts.

3. When the Holy Spirit controls a Christian, he is not carried away nor out of control as the idolaters were.

4. The Holy Spirit does not exalt Himself but exalts Christ as Lord.

Paul now deals with the source of gifts.

II. UNITY OF SOURCE AND PURPOSE IN THE DIVERSITY OF GIFTS, 12:4-11

Source of gifts. "Now there are diversities of gifts, but the same spirit," (v. 4). The text brings in the word *gifts* which is *charismata.* In verse 1 it was the "spirituals" (essence and source). Here it is the "gifts" (endowments for ministry).

Throughout this passage the source of the gifts is God. "It is the same God which worketh all in all," (v. 6). "The same Lord" is mentioned in verse 5. Besides God the Father and God the Son, God the Holy Spirit is referred to particularly as the source of spiritual gifts. Note verses 1, 4, 7, 8 (twice), 9 (twice), and 11. The *charismata* are "by the same spirit" and "worketh that one and the self-same spirit".

Unity. All of this is *unity in diversity,* a unity in relationship to the Trinity. The Holy Spirit gives the gifts. The Son of God assigns the place of the ministry of the gifts in the body. The Father provides the energy in the outworking of the gifts. The whole Godhead is involved in these gifts and in the place of service for these gifts.

The entire Trinity is the source of the gifts, a unity of source.

When one uses his gift as God intended, it provides unity among believers, not division. Here is the answer in part to one of the Corinthian problems—division. Used as God designs, true spiritual gifts bring Christians together. They do not drive them apart!

Diversity. In the original the first word of verse 4 is "diversities". Here we see *diversity in unity.* Verses 4 to 6 bring this emphasis. "There are diversities of gifts," "there are differences (diversities) of administrations," "and there are diversities of operations." In all the diversity the Holy Spirit seeks to preserve unity.

Romans 12:6-9 and Ephesians 4:7-16 give other lists of the gifts of the Spirit besides those before us in chapter 12:8-10 and 12:28-30. All told there are at least eighteen different gifts of the Holy Spirit. Nine gifts of the Spirit are before us in 12:8-10, and eight are listed in 12:28. Each Christian has at least one or more of these gifts.

In this study we are concerned only with speaking in tongues and their interpretation, but notice the diversity in unity! Even in the days of the Corinthian Church, tongues were not everything!

Sovereign bestowal. We have noted that there is unity in diversity because the gifts are from one God. We have also noted that there is diversity in unity. Many gifts are at hand. Paul then declares, "But the manifestation of the Spirit is given to every man to profit withal," (v. 7). Every Christian man, woman, youth, boy or girl receives a gift of the Spirit for profit. "To another . . . " is repeated eight times in verses 8-10. The summary of the work of the Holy spirit appears in verse 11 as he "divides to every man severally (individually) as He will."

Every believer receives his gift or gifts from God by sovereign bestowal at the moment of salvation. This refers to spiritual gifts, not natural gifts. He already has his spiritual gift(s). He does not have to pray, or plead, fast or weep, or do anything else to receive his gifts. These are already given, but we are responsible to discover and to use them.

Each believer has at least one gift. Some have more than one. These gifts are given as He determines, not as the individual believer determines. The Christian is not to review the gifts as one might look over coats or suits at a local department store and think, "I want that one!" He does not have that right. The Holy Spirit decides.

Therefore, to seek the gift of tongues would amount to giving orders to God about an area which is His and His alone to decide. The Word states, "as He will," (v. 11), not as we want.

"Charismatic" or "non-charismatic" has come to be the identifying label for one who either speaks in tongues or does not speak in tongues. Though we must live apparently with such a popular designation, the term is not technically correct. Some of those who speak in tongues are not charismatic since they otherwise give no evidence of knowing Christ as personal Savior. On the other hand, in view of these verses, whether or not one speaks in tongues, *every Christian is a charismatic* because he or she possesses one or more gifts! Praise God, the Holy Spirit gives His gifts to *every* Christian "as He will"!

The Corinthians had been preoccupied with *one* particular manifestation of the Spirit—speaking in tongues—which brought divisions. By speaking of the unity of source and the great diversity of the gifts, Paul was trying to get the Corinthians to see the variety of the Spirit's working. Twentieth century Christians would do well to observe this pattern, too.

Speaking in tongues is *last* in the list of verses 8-10, and also *last* in the list of verses 28-30 where rank is definitely stated.

If we begin where the Scriptures begin, we will never end in the Corinthian extravagance.

CHAPTER SEVEN

Many Yet One
(Read I Corinthians 12:12-31)

Forty-five thousand French-speaking Catholic charismatics met in the Olympic stadium in Montreal in June, 1977, for the final meeting of a two-day conference. It was the largest religious gathering in Quebec in more than ten years. Nine hundred priests, eight bishops, and an archbishop held a three and one-half hour mass during the meeting. In July of the same year, forty-five thousand U.S. charismatics from dozens of denominations met in Kansas City, Missouri, for a conference on charismatic renewal. Such conferences are illustrative of continuing charismatic interest.[1]

In the opening verses of chapter 12 the great test of utterance emphasized the vital importance of the lordship of Jesus Christ. The triune God appeared as the source of the *charismata*, the gifts, of great diversity and balance and sovereignly bestowed.

In the last half of chapter 12 the diversities of the gifts in one body are emphasized: "Many yet one"!

I. RELATIONSHIP OF MEMBERS OF THE BODY TO EACH OTHER, 12:12-27

Body illustration. The apostle uses the human body as an illustration of the body of Christ and of the gifts of the members of that body. "For as the body is one, and hath many members, and all the members of that one body, being many, are one body: so also is Christ," (v. 12). The human body is one and has many members. The spiritual body, called the church in Ephesians 1:22-23 and Colossians 1:18, also is one and has many members. Many members yet one body! In the last part of the verse, the rendering is (lit.) "so also *the* Christ!"

Christ is the central One and He has many members. The body of Christ and individual believers as members of that living, spiritual organism are before us.

Baptism by the Holy Spirit. The apostle explains the method of belonging. "For by one Spirit are we all baptized into one body, whether we be Jews or Gentiles, whether we be bond or free; and have been all made to drink into one Spirit," (v. 13). As explained in the second chapter, the baptism of the Holy Spirit places believers into the great body of Christ and joins them to the head of that body.

The "for" at the beginning of this verse shows that the comparison with the human body is correct because all believers have been baptized into one spiritual body. The word "are" of the King James Version should really be translated "were", i.e. "by one Spirit *were* all baptized into one body." Paul is not considering a present experience, but a past event in the lives of the Corinthian Christians. Furthermore, he is bringing out the fact that the baptism of the Holy Spirit is true of *all* the Corinthian believers, no matter the background. This is true of *every* believer today! It is true of you if you are a Christian, no matter the racial or social background or even the quality of your walk with the Lord.

Paul's contrast is enlightening, "Now if any man have not the Spirit of Christ, he is none of his," (Rom. 8:9b).

Body relationship. But it is not only essential to be in the body. The members of the body must be seen in their relationship *to the body* and *to each other*, vv. 14ff. Every member is in the body and yet every member has a relationship to every other member in that body.

Members of the body are mutually necessary and dependent upon one another.

Isn't that amazing? The body is one with Christ as the head. You and I as believers are members of that body. We are necessary in that body, no matter how feeble nor how prominent, and we are dependent upon each other!

God is the Designer-Creator and He alone determines what place and function each member shall have. Three verses lend support. "But *now hath God set* the members every one of them in the body, as it hath pleased Him," (v. 18), "but *God hath tempered* the body together," (v. 24), "and *God hath set* some in the church . . .," (v. 28).

The reason why God set the members in place or tempered the body together is disclosed in verses 25 and 26, "that there should be no schism in the body; but that the members should have the same care one for another. And whether one member suffer, all the members suffer with it; or one member be honored, all the members rejoice with it." The members of the spiritual body of Christ are mutually necessary and dependent upon one another. This care and mutual respect prevents schism or division of that body.

It is ridiculous for one jealous member to say it is not of the body because it does not happen to be another particular member. "If the foot shall say, because I am not the hand, I am not of the body; is it therefore not of the body? And if the ear shall say, because I am not the eye, I am not of the body; is it therefore not of the body? If the whole body were an eye, where were the hearing? If the whole were hearing, where were the smelling?" (vv. 15-17). Sister ear, for example, might feel inferior because she was not brother eye! But she is still in the body.

How foolish for the less admired members to seek to be the more admired ones or to declare no need of each other. "And the eye cannot say unto the hand, I have no need of thee: nor again the head to the feet, I have no need of you. Nay, much more those members of the body, which seem to be more feeble, are necessary: and those members of the body, which we think to be less honourable, upon these we bestow more abundant honour; and our uncomely parts have more abundant comeliness," (vv. 21-23).

God may give you more than one gift in the body, but you should not jealously seek the gift of another member. God did not intend the whole body to have the same gift. The charismatic movement seems to say that the body should be all tongue. In view of this Scripture, it would be, and is, sin to start a movement that centers on one gift such as a "tongues movement!"

Gardiner describes it this way, "Imagine, if you can, an ear saying, 'No one ever looks longingly unto me and comments on how beautiful I am, like they do the eyes. I will seek to be an eye'. So the poor ear fasts and prays, prostrates itself, pores out its wax, seeking to be a eye. How ridiculous! An ear is an ear. God made it an ear and placed it on the side of the head. If it succeeded in changing into an eye, the body would be handicapped with poor hearing and embarrassed by three eyes."[2]

The whole point is that God has sovereignly given gifts and placed the gifted people as He desires, not as they desire. Here is a truth for the physical body, but also a truth for the spiritual body of Christ.

Near the conclusion of the chapter Paul asks these questions, "Are all apostles? Are all prophets? Are all teachers? Are all workers of miracles? Have all the gifts of healing? Do all speak with tongues? Do all interpret?" (vv. 29-30). According to Greek usage, all of these questions require "no" for an answer! Do all speak with tongues? *No!* Do all interpret? *No!*

How contrary to the Scripture to teach, therefore, that all believers should seek for the gift of tongues to prove that they have been baptized with the Holy Ghost and are members of the body of Christ! After all, not every believer would have the gift of speaking in tongues nor the gift of interpretation!

Sometimes charismatics turn to Mark 16:15-20 to support their platform that the gift of speaking in tongues is for every Christian. "And these signs shall follow them that believe; in my name shall they cast out devils; they shall speak with new (i.e. new to the speaker—foreign languages) tongues! they shall take up serpents; and if they drink any deadly thing, it shall not hurt them; they shall lay hands on the sick, and they shall recover," (vv. 17-18). These verses were spoken to the apostles who believed. It is a mistake to suppose that the signs always and continually followed those who believed the messengers.

If we accept verse 17 for today, we must also accept verse 18a for today. "They shall take up serpents; and if they drink any deadly thing, it shall not hurt them." Are spiritual Christians prepared for this? Can one be faithful in interpretation by sorting out for today what they want in a context, but rejecting another part of it?

The key is found in verse 20. "And they went forth, and preached everywhere, the Lord working with them, and confirming the Word with signs following. Amen." The great commission and the reaction of verses 15 and 16 still stand, but the signs were confirmatory signs to the early church. The gospel message of the apostles was confirmed by these signs before the New Testament was written. After the New Testament was written, there was no further need for these signs.

To say that the gift of speaking in tongues is for everyone on the basis of Mark 16, therefore, is not justified.

Corinthian trouble. The church at Corinth had been

seeking showy gifts which would bring attention to themselves. In particular, they had been seeking tongues, *the lesser* of the gifts. They were sensational, dramatic, showy, *but lesser.*

In verse 31a, Paul states in contrast, "But covet earnestly the best gifts." The verb is in plural form. Paul is referring to them as a church. "Seek or desire earnestly" *the greater gifts, not the lesser.* Some strain the translation of verse 31a and miss the point of the context by using the indicative mode (simple statement), though the form would permit it. "But you are seeking earnestly the best gifts."[3] The word "best" must be rendered "showy" for this rendering to have any meaning. The word in the original, however, is "greater". The Corinthians were not earnestly seeking the greater gifts! Expositor Albert Barnes rightly comments, ". . . there is no valid objection to the common translation in the imperative (command), and indeed the connection seems to demand it."[4]

In contrast to the lesser gift which the Corinthians had been seeking, Paul requests them to seek earnestly the greater. The revelation of the greater unfolds in chapter 14 and is identified as prophecy. Note verse 1, "Follow after charity (or love), and desire spiritual gifts, but rather that ye may prophesy." The verb "desire" is the same word and form as "covet" of 12:31a. "Seek eagerly the spirituals, but rather in order that you might prophesy." Prophecy is the greater.

God sovereignly bestows gifts to individual members of the assembly, but *as a church* the desire should be for the greater of these gifts by way of emphasis.

One might ask why consideration of the word "covet" is important. Because some are saying, "Covet tongues today. Seek to speak in tongues". God's sovereign bestowal of gifts has already answered this challenge as improper. But note the usage.

The word "covet" is used five times in the immediate context (12:31; 13:4; 14:1, 12, 39). In the love chapter (13:4) the meaning is "burn with envy". In the other uses the meaning is "seek eagerly" with the form either indicative or imperative. The context must determine which is to be used. We have already looked at 12:31 and 14:1. In 14:12 the word "zealous" may be rendered "to seek eagerly". In 14:39 "covet" again means "to seek eagerly", the latter with regard to prophecy. In none of these passages are we commanded or even urged to seek to speak in tongues. Paul is saying "the greater" (prophecy) is better, surpassing speaking in tongues.

II. RANK OF THE GIFTS AND OF THE CHRISTIANS WITH GIFTS, 12:28-31a

Rank of the gifts. The list of the gifts also contributes to the argument of the superiority of prophecy over tongues. "And God hath set some in the church, first apostles, secondarily prophets, thirdly teachers, after that miracles, then gifts of healing, helps, governments, and diversities of tongues," (12:28).

Numbering the gifts listed in this verse indicates that the gifts are listed in order of importance. A descending order is intended. First in importance are apostles, prophets, and teachers. Tongues are placed at the bottom of the list.

Paul was intimating that if you are determined to seek a gift, do not seek tongues. Instead seek one of the greater gifts, one closer to the top of the list.

Paul's continual aim is maturity over immaturity and the greater over the lesser!

Rank of Christians with gifts. Some charismatics have displayed "super-righteousness" and have claimed that because of their speaking in tongues they were Spirit-filled Christians, while others were just "ordinary" Christians.

In Paul's day there was a parallel to this outlook. Paul wrote to the Church in Colosse to refute a group called Gnostics, who plagued the church during the latter part of the first century and subsequently.

These Gnostics claimed to be the recepients of a higher knowledge, *gnosis*, that enabled them to walk in a more intimate union with God than others. They placed a special emphasis on mystical "spiritual" experiences.

There are at least two parallels between ancient gnosticism and the modern charismatic movement.[5] First, they distinguished between what they called the pneumatic or Spirit-filled Christian, with levels in between based on "higher experiences", and the psychic or ordinary Christian. The so-called pneumatic Christians considered themselves to be on a higher level and were more mystical and more "spiritual" than others. The parallel rests between the spiritual charismatics and the "ordinary" Christians today.

Secondly, the Gnostics maintained that the evidence of whether you have become pneumatic (more spiritual) consisted of certain "miraculous" and "higher" experiences. This was central in many of the pagan mystery religions. In these cults, speaking in tongues was an evidence that one had moved up to a higher state. So, like Gnosticism, with the modern charismatic movement. One moves up spiritually when he or she experiences the "baptism, tongues, etc.".

Paul countered the Gnostic influence in various ways. "For this cause, we also since the day we heard it, do not cease to pray for you, to desire that you might be filled with the knowledge of His will in all wisdom and spiritual understanding: that ye might walk worthy of the Lord unto all pleasing, being fruitful in every good work, and increasing in the knowledge of God," (Col. 1:9-10). The Gnostics boasted knowlege. Paul offered "full knowledge" *(epignosis)*.

Paul spoke of Christ's headship, of His pre-eminence in all things, that all fullness dwelt in Him, (Col. 1:18-19). Paul desired to "present every man perfect in Christ Jesus," (1:28). Paul longed for their "acknowledgement (full knowledge) of the mystery of God, even Christ," (2:2b).

In Colossians 2:9-10, Paul intimates that nothing can be added to completeness. "For in Him dwelleth all the fulness of the God-head bodily and ye are complete in Him, which is the head of all principality and power."

In Gnosticism the highest form of the spiritual life was inward, self-edifying. So with the modern charismatic. In contrast, Paul's challenge of chapter 14 is to edify the church, and in chapter 13 to love other Christians, not display superiority of spirit over them.

The Colossians were being tempted to look for "fulness" beyond Christ. Paul stresses that they already have the fullness because *they are in Christ.*

Recently Dr. John G. Mitchell, founder and professor at Multnomah School of the Bible in Portland, Oregon, told how he was approached by certain charismatic teachers. Dr. Mitchell asked them, "Would you say that I am a Christian?" "Oh, yes," they said, "we believe you are a Christian." "Then," said Dr. Mitchell, "do you believe that Jesus is living in me?" "Yes, of course, we do!" was their answer. Then Dr. Mitchell said to them, "If I have Christ, I have everything!"

Paul said it in another way, "Blessed be the God and Father of our Lord Jesus Christ, who hath blessed us with all spiritual blessings in heavenly places in Christ," (Eph. 1:3). Is it logically possible to look for more once one has received *all* or every spiritual blessing?

The believer already has everything. Absolutely nothing can be added. We may need to appropriate more of what we already have in Him, grow, and become more mature, but *in Christ I have everything now.*

In the first century any teaching of a "fullness beyond Christ" such as the Gnostics offered was viewed as heresy. What should it be called today?

An aged silver miner had spent all his life searching for silver in the mountains of the old West. He had become so obsessed with his search that his wife and his children had left him. When he died, the handful of people who came to bury him found in his possession a note instructing them to bury him under his cabin. As the spades full of earth were turned over, a lustrous gray material began to appear. It was the famous Comstock Silver Vein, the richest in Nevada's history. That miner had been a theoretical millionaire much of his life, but he had never claimed nor recognized his wealth.

Likewise, many believers are spiritual billionaires, but seldom claim the blessing God has for them. Every person who is in Christ has everything God can ever give him. The question is, "Will we claim God's promises by faith and begin living them in our daily walk?" Someone has said, "Stop clamoring and start claiming."[6]

We are "many yet one". Yes, many members, yet one body! The relationship of diversity and mutual help and rank of the gifts encourages the church to seek earnestly the greater gifts rather than speaking in tongues!

CHAPTER EIGHT

True Love and the Charismatic

(Read I Corinthians 13:1-13)

One of the greatest chapters in the Bible is I Corinthians 13, often called the Love Chapter. Thousands of messages have been based on this outstanding, lofty passage. It is right that this is so.

What is often forgotten, however, is this chapter's immediate context. Never forget that chapter 13 is between chapter 12 and chapter 14! It does not stand alone. It is the very heart of Paul's teaching about the spiritual life and is absolutely essential to the truth of chapters 12 and 14.

The whole speaks of the "spirituals," (12:1)—things whose essence is spiritual and whose source is the Holy Spirit. The *principles* regarding spiritual gifts appear in chapter 12. While the *exercise* of the gifts highlights chapter 14, chapter 13 accents the *spirit* of the ministry of the gifts. Chapter 13 *guards* against making these gifts in themselves the supreme object of life, which belongs to love personified in Jesus Christ. Early verses really provide a description of Christ and "a more excellent way" introduced in I Cor. 12:31b, "And yet I show to you a way *beyond measure.*"

The phrase translated "more excellent" in our Authorized Version does not carry the impact intended in the original. "Beyond measure" is better. That phrase is used at least four times by Paul *(kath huperbolain):* Romans 7:13; I Corinthians 12:31; II Corinthians 1:8; Galatians 1:13.

What is the way "beyond measure" which Paul longed to show to the Corinthians and that the Lord longs to show to us? It is love! It is the greatest, (13:13c)!

Throughout this chapter the apostle talks about the highest kind of love, the *agape* "God-like kind". There are six occurrences of this word in the chapter, though the whole is of that love.

Here is the truly spiritual life, a life controlled by the Spirit of God as evidenced by the fruit of the Spirit, not the gifts of the Spirit. The apostle uses the first and all-embracing fruit of love as the standard.

The fruit are listed in Galatians 5:22-23, "But the fruit of the Spirit is love, joy, peace, longsuffering, gentleness, goodness, faith, meekness, temperance: against such there is no law."

Love is first in that list. It can be readily seen that when God's love really controls my life there will also be joy, peace, patience, gentleness, meekness, and the rest of the fruit. Thus Paul uses the fruit of the Spirit, love, to describe the life controlled by the Holy Spirit.

I. PRIORITY OF LOVE, vv. 1-3

At least six gifts of the Spirit are referred to in the first three verses of I Corinthians 13. "Though I speak with the tongues (languages) of men and of angels (who bring a message from God), and have not charity, I am become as sounding brass, or a tinkling symbol. And though I have the gift of prophecy, and understand all mysteries, and all knowledge; and though I have all faith, so that I could remove mountains, and have not charity, I am nothing. And though I bestow all my goods to feed the poor, and though I give my body to be burned, and have not charity, it profiteth me nothing."

These six gifts may refer to the gift of speaking in tongues, the gift of prophecy, the gift of understanding mysteries (which suggests the "word of wisdom" of 12:8 or the "discerning of spirits" of 12:10), the gift of knowledge, and the gift of faith. Verse 3 might speak of the gift of ministry or giving or showing mercy as in Romans 12:6-8, or even the "helps" of 12:28.

All of these are excellent gifts, but if they are exercised without the fruit of the Spirit, without love, they are worthless.

Tongues, *the lesser gift*, prophecy, *the greater gift* (mentioned consecutively for emphasis), knowledge, faith, mercy, even self-sacrifice add up to zero when the life is not producing spiritual fruit, especially love.

What are the results of pursuing the gifts of the Spirit without the fruit of the Spirit which is love? Paul spells it out. I merely clang. *I give out nothing,* v. 1b! *I am nothing,* v. 2! *It profits me nothing,* v. 3! The suggestion of the wrong motive of personal glory may be inferred in this verse, too.

It is very important to notice that Paul is saying here that it is possible to have gifts and no spirituality. Spiritual gifts and spirituality are not synonymous! In addition, he is clearly telling his readers that spiritual gifts do not produce spirituality. This insight has already been illustrated graphically by the low spiritual life among the Corinthians who had ALL the gifts.

You and I may or may not speak with tongues or even manifest some other spiritual gifts in our lives, but we need *more love.*

Mr. Murray, the publisher, said that every time Tennyson's poems were printed, an extra supply of the letters "l" and "v" had to be purchased because the poet used the word "love" so often in his compositions. May love hold a similar place in the poem of our life, for it is the believer's trademark! Love is to have priority!

II. POWER OF LOVE, vv. 4-7

Paul turns from the negative to the positive in verse 4. Love is the quality of life which will be produced when the Christian is controlled by the Holy Spirit. "Charity suffereth long and is kind; charity envieth not; charity vaunteth not itself, is not puffed up". Love does not quit. It is not spasmodic. It is not turned on and off. It is kind.

Love does not "burn with envy". We need to remember that envy was the Corinthian trouble pointed out by the ridiculous illustrations of the human body in chapter 12. The ear wanted to be an eye, etc.

The Corinthians were whispering, "I want his gift. He speaks in tongues. He prophesies. All I can do is to administer or show mercy. I want what he has." Paul says, "love envies not"!

"Love vaunteth not itself, is not puffed up," (v. 4c). Love does not "boast nor vaunt itself". Love is not self-seeking.

In chapters 12 and 14 Paul points out that the body should be the first concern, not the individual's personal desires. "The members should have the same care one for another," (12:25b). The apostle discourages tongues as a tool of self-edification and encourages prophecy because it produces the edification and comfort of others, (14:3-4).

The Corinthians were proud of their gifts. They looked with disdain on those who had not received the "baptism" with the so-called initial sign of speaking in tongues. They were not displaying love.

Love "doth not behave itself unseemly," (v. 5a). This is the only New Testament use of this word. Love is never indecent nor out of control. It does not produce the improper.

Gardiner says, "For over twenty years of this writer's life, I was associated with charismatic churches. I saw women 'slain under the power,' sprawled on the floor while the altar workers tugged at their skirts or covered them with 'altar clothes' and coats to minimize the indecent exposure! Is it not inconceivable that the Holy Spirit would be a party to indecent exposure? Love does not behave itself unseemly. This sentence, coupled with the one about their having been out of control when they were pagans (12:2) is a powerful warning. God is not the author of confusion (14:33) nor of indecent behaviour and, when these are present, they are not of the Holy Spirit."[1]

"Love is not provoked nor roused to anger. Love thinks no evil," (v. 5bc). It does not impute evil to others and try to judge their motives. Love "does not rejoice in iniquity," (v. 6a). Love "rejoices in the truth," (v. 6b). Love "beareth all things," (v. 7a). This means that love "bears up under pressure." Another use nearer the root meaning of this word in the original is "to cover, to keep secret, to conceal".

Remember the old adage, "Love covers a multitude of sins." How like our Lord Jesus! When we come to Him in faith, His great love does just that. Through His precious work at Calvary He puts a "ceiled roof" over our sins. Actually the concealing is so great that He not only forgives but "as far as the east is from the west, so far hath He *removed* our transgressions from us," (Psalm 103:12). That's remote concealing of the best kind!

In the seventh verse the word *all* is first in every case, with only the verb following. Love as the subject is inferred. All things love bears. All things love believes. All things love hopes. All things love endures. How great the power of true love!

Love bears all things, but not without a purpose. Love believes all things, but not gullibly—always on the basis of facts. Love hopes all things—not with wishful thinking, but resting on God's promises. Love endures all things, not blindly but with a look to Him and to eternity.

Love may be compared to light passing through a prism. When we allow light to pass through a prism, a beautiful spectrum of colors unfolds in all its glory. As with light so with love. Love is made up of many things, many facets of the beauty of character, especially exemplified in the glory of the beauty of character of our Lord Jesus Christ. Try reading verses 4 through 7, substituting "Christ" for "love" in each case!

III. PERMANENCE OF LOVE, vv. 8-10

One of the greatest characteristics of love is that it is permanent. Paul contrasts love with that which is temporary. "Love never fails," (v. 8a). Love never falls to ruin nor destruction. It lasts forever. Love always abides, (v. 13).

The fruit of the Spirit is lasting. Love, being a fruit is therefore lasting. Paul says to the Corinthian Church, "Here is something which will last. Gifts are good, but some may be temporary. They may be made inactive or even cease. Love lasts! This must be the spirit of the exercise of your gifts." Love must also be the spirit in exercising our gifts today.

IV. PRINCIPLE OF MATURITY IN LOVE, vv. 11-12

Growth is a process. One should see a difference between the beginning of that process and farther down the road. "When I was a child, I spake as a child, I understood as a child, I thought as a child; but when I became a man, I put away childish things," (v. 11).

Paul is saying, "Childhood is a time of immaturity. You speak, understand, and think like a child." Five times in this one short verse he refers to childhood and its immaturity. When you reach maturity, however, you make childish things inactive in your experience.

The verbs in the last part of verse 11 are in the Greek

perfect tense. This is action completed in the past which continues completed in the present. "I became a man in the past. I am still a man. I have put away childish, infant things in the past. They are still put away."

Paul's implied cry is, "My dear brethren in Corinth, I want you to be mature and "maturity is the growth produced in you by the Holy Spirit over a period of time."[2] That growth will be evidenced in the fruit of the Spirit which is love.

Therefore, tongues, which are so important to many people today, just as they were in the infancy of the early church, are not the evidence needed for maturity. Possessing the gift of speaking in tongues will not bring maturity.

Grow up! Become mature! "Make inactive" the things of your childhood!

This thought may be tied in with I Cor. 14:20, "Brethren, be not children in understanding; howbeit in malice be ye children, but in understanding be men." Do not be children in understanding. In malice be babes (infants), for infants do not bear ill will! In understanding be mature, *teleioi*. The over-all impact is clear. Do not hang on to the things of childhood when you should be moving on to the things of maturity.

True love is a part of that maturity. Show it. Exercise it!

V. CONCLUSION REGARDING LOVE, v. 13

Love is the greatest! This is the way "beyond measure," the fruit of the Spirit. "Love is what I want to see in your life," states Paul.

Speaking in tongues is worthless without love. If one's attitude is self-seeking and proud, love is not seen nor is Christ honored. Spiritual maturity is desired. Tongues will not bring this. True love in Christ will.

Fond parents often say to a little child, "How much do you love me?" The answer is usually a hug and a kiss. If you put the same question to our Heavenly Father, the answer is—the cross! We can only glimpse the sufferings of Christ in the Garden, and on Calvary, but we cannot know the fullness of the Father's love in that hour!

CHAPTER NINE

Tongues
A Temporary Gift?

(Read I Corinthians 13:8-13)

Is speaking in tongues for today or is speaking in tongues a temporary gift? This is the crucial question people are asking.

Again, the Christian's evaluating standard must be *"what saith the Scripture"*, not experience.

I. TONGUES SHALL CEASE, 13:8b

The Scriptures teach that tongues will one day be stilled. "Charity never faileth: but whether there be prophecies, they shall fail; whether there be tongues, they shall cease; whether there be knowledge, it shall vanish away," (13:8).

Permanent love is contrasted against things of a less permanent nature. "Love never fails." On the other hand, prophecies, tongues, and knowledge present a different story.

What does verse 8 really say? The Greek verb (*katargeo*) is used four times in this chapter and is important to the meaning of this verse. *Katargeo*, translated, means "to make inactive".

Verse 8 is actually saying, "whether there be prophecies, they *shall be made inactive.*" "Whether there be knowledge, it *shall be made inactive.*" The same verb appears in verse 10, "then that which is in part *shall be made inactive.*" Every occurrence of this verb in verses 8 and 10 is in the passive voice indicating that someone (God) shall make prophecy, knowledge, and "that which is in part" inactive. The fourth use of *katargeo* in verse 11 has the active voice and is not pertinent.

The verb "to make inactive" is used with both prophecy and knowledge, but the verb used with tongues is different. "Whether there be tongues, they shall cease (*pauomai*)". The thought is that they will do this "in and of themselves". The verb appears in the middle voice indicating that tongues would die out of their own accord.

Thus Paul does not link prophecy, tongues, and knowledge together in their cessation as some believe. One often hears it said, "If tongues have ceased, then knowledge must have ceased, too. We know that knowledge is still here; therefore tongues must still be here."[1]

The simple answer is that knowledge refers to special revelation as a gift (12:8) and is *not* still here in that primary sense. Thus tongues need not be here on that premise either.

The question is, "When will prophecy and knowledge be made inactive?" The repeated phrase "in part" of verse 9 helps disclose the answer. The apostle further links together prophecy and knowledge by saying, "For we know in part, and we prophecy in part."

Paul continues in verse 10, "But when that which is perfect is come, then that which is in part shall be done away." What was "in part"? Knowledge and prophecy! Paul is saying that when that which is perfect comes, knowledge and prophecy shall be made inactive! Remember that the words "done away" really come from our key word *katargeo*, "to make inactive".

When will "that which is perfect" come in order that knowledge and prophecy may be made inactive? To make heaven the answer is to miss the flow of Paul's argument to the Corinthian Church. Dr. Roy L. Laurin in his commentary on I Corinthians says, "This perfection is the perfection of maturity. Paul speaks later of being a child and of becoming a man," (v. 11). Therefore, the things of the early age of Christianity's immaturity would be supplanted by the things of Christianity's maturity. He deliberately states that the partial shall be done away. This means that there will no longer be any use for them. They will have served their purpose. They will fulfill the time of divine intention."[2] To this Dillow agrees.[3]

These things are the gifts of prophecy (foretelling) and knowledge (special revelation) in their primary sense. *They shall be made inactive!*

Verse 12 then links the "growth to maturity" principle of the Corinthian day to the ultimate in Christ's presence. "For now we see through a glass darkly; but then face to face: now I know in part; but then shall I know even as also I am known."

Paul states that now we see through a glass or "in a mirror in an enigma dimly". The Corinthians would understand this comparison because their local art had developed a means of polishing metal to a fair degree of reflection. Their homes were full of mirrors, but they were imperfect mirrors, not like our silver-backed kind. Looking into their mirrors, they saw themselves "darkly".[4]

So it was with these gifts of prophecy and knowledge. "Now I know in part." Paul says, "Some day it will be different!" "Face to face" — God's face and my face! Then I shall know others and will know all mysteries even as God knows me now and has known me all through the years. The church will then move "into full maturity" in the ultimate sense.[5]

What about tongues? Paul only states here that they would cease in and of themselves, verse 8. When? When did tongues cease? The intimation is that their cessation came at this time of the church's growth to maturity.

The answer, however, does not depend upon one verse alone, but rather is based on the whole of Biblical revelation as seen in the following.

II. EVIDENCE THAT THE GIFT OF TONGUES CEASED IN THE FIRST CENTURY

Joseph Dillow in his book *Speaking In Tongues* presents five different categories of evidence to support the temporary aspect of the gift of tongues. His categories are used in the following pages.[6]

Factors Relating to God's Covenant Relationship to Israel. According to the ancient prophets, God will one day establish a global kingdom in fulfillment of His promise to David (I Chron. 17:11-15; Isa. 2:1-5; 9:6-7, etc.).

The miraculous will be the common daily experiences of believers in this kingdom. Men will live hundreds of years (Isa. 65:20). Wolves and lambs will feed together. (Isa. 65:25). Furthermore, it will be an unparalleled age of the fullness of the Spirit (Isa. 32:15; 35:1-6; 41:1; Jer. 31:33; Joel 2, etc.).

Continuous miracles, however, in the Bible are the exception and always are connected with God fulfilling His promise to the Jews. There are only three major outbreaks of miracles in the Scriptures: (1) Moses and Joshua (1441-1370 B.C.), (2) Elijah and Elisha (870-785 B.C.), and (3) Christ and the Apostles (28-70 A.D.).

Fig. 2 "MAJOR OUTBREAKS OF BIBLICAL MIRACLES"

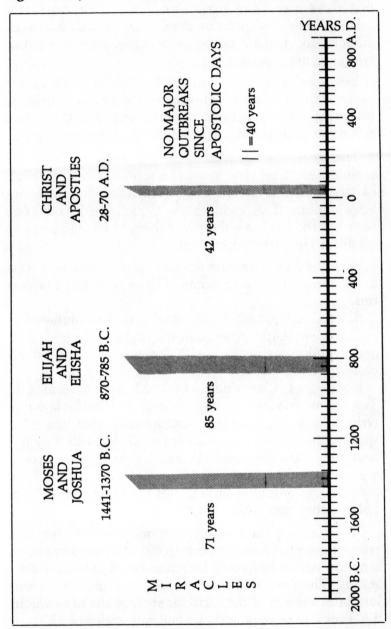

In each major outbreak, miracles were needed to prove that these men were from God. Once their work was accomplished the continuous miracles ceased. Scattered miracles for specific purposes occurred, but it was not God's normal operation.

Yes, God performs miracles today, but not as the norm. The charismatic movement claims that miracles, including tongues, should be the norm. The Bible does not show that, excluding the miracle of the new birth.

Therefore, the miracles of the first century, including tongues, must be viewed as a temporary break-through of that future kingdom and not a norm for this non-kingdom age. This includes the miracles of Jesus in one sense, as the Jews saw them and thought He had come to establish His earthly kingdom.

Even the Acts 2 tongues miracle Peter connected with a break-through of the kingdom. The tie with Joel 2 proves this.

Since God's judgment on Israel was consummated in A.D. 70, we might expect that the "break-through" signs and wonders associated with Israel's kingdom would cease by then, also.

Consider I Corinthians 14:21-22 and several Old Testament passages relating to tongues. "In the law it is written, with men of other tongues and other lips will I speak unto this people: and yet for all that will they not hear me, saith the Lord. Wherefore tongues are for a sign, not to them that believe, but to them that believe not: but prophesying serveth not for them that believe not but for them which believe."

"Tongues are for a sign." The quotation of verse 21 refers in part to Deuteronomy 28:49 with its judgment by a nation whose tongue or language Israel did not understand. "The Lord shall bring a nation against thee from far, from the end of the earth, as swift as the eagle flieth; a nation whose tongue thou shalt not understand."

Consider also the promise of Jeremiah 5:11, 15. "For the house of Israel and the house of Judah have dealt very treacherously against me, saith the Lord . . . Lo, I will bring a nation upon you from far, O house of Israel, saith the Lord! it is a mighty nation, it is an ancient nation, a nation whose language thou knowest not, neither understandest what they say."

Even more pertinent is Isaiah 28:11-12, where the Assyrian captivity is in view. "For with stammering lips and another tongue will he speak to this people. To whom he said, this is the rest wherewith ye may cause the weary to rest; and this is the refreshing: yet they would not hear."

Compare also Isaiah 33:19 where the absence of foreign tongues is a sign that the nation is under the blessing of God!

Including the Bible's first reference to tongues in Genesis 11 (Tower of Babel), George W. Zeller traces a uniform four-fold sequence and pattern in these references and their context: (1) God's message, (2) the people's refusal to listen, (3) tongues heard as a sign of judgment, and (4) dispersion.[7] Therefore, except for Genesis 11 in the above cases, tongues were primarily historically *a judicial sign against Jewish unbelief* as a nation.

Paul applies the same to Corinth. Walter R. Bodine is right. Paul "has lifted the Jewish unbelief of Isaiah 28:12 from its original setting and applied it to his own day."[8] "This people" of I Corinthians 14:21 are the Jews. "They" of v. 21 continues to refer to the Jews. In v. 22 tongues are a sign to "them that believe not", still referring to the Jews.

There were Jews at Corinth who did not believe. The gift of tongues was a judicial sign against Jewish unbelief in that place.

With the destruction of Jerusalem in A.D. 70, the sign significance of the gift ended. The gift that was uniquely for a sign of that judgment was no longer needed. After the judgment, the sign must have passed from the church.

Factors Relating to the Foundation Period of the Church. As already noted, I Corinthians 13:8, 11 relate the gift of tongues to the infancy period of the church when tongues would cease as the church became mature. They would die out in and of themselves.

Dillow says, "Therefore, the childhood of the church ended when the existence of Israel as a nation ended. Then there was no longer any need for a sign to *authenticate* the insignificant church, nor for a *sign against* the extinct Jewish nation".[9] (italics mine).

The foundation period of the church had apostles and prophets as Ephesians 2:20 states. "Ye," referring to the church, "are built on the foundation of the apostles and prophets." This refers to New Testament apostles and prophets.

The gift of apostleship passed in part because of the requirements for its possession. One must have seen Jesus alive after the resurrection (I Cor. 9:1) to qualify for an apostle in the primary sense.

The supernatural gift of the prophet in the primary sense also passed when the New Testament was completed. There was no further need for additional revelation.

It could be demonstrated that the gifts of miracles, and of healing — note we said *gifts* — also were temporary gifts. Of course God still performs miracles and heals as He chooses in answer to prayer.

Since other gifts of the foundation period are temporary gifts, then there follows the strong probability that tongues — a lesser gift — could also be temporary.

Factors Relating to the Closing of the Canon. The

basic argument here rests with the fact that the gift of tongues was a necessary gift, along with the other gifts given for divine revelation, during the time when the church had no New Testament in written form.

Once the New Testament had been written, the need for these gifts passed, and therefore the gifts, including tongues also probably passed from the church.

"God, who at sundry times and in divers manners spake in time past unto the fathers by the prophets, hath in these last days spoken unto us by his Son, whom he hath appointed heir of all things, by whom also He made the worlds," (Heb. 1:1-2). God once *spoke* to the fathers by the prophets. But now He *has spoken* to us in His Son. He is *not speaking by tongues, but by Son* today!

Factors Relating to the Authentication of Christ and His Apostles. One of the major purposes of the gift of tongues and the other miraculous gifts in the first century was to verify that Christ was God and that His apostles were the messengers of the new era.

It is never said of Christ that He spoke in tongues, but that gift authenticated the messengers and the message concerning Him as declared by His apostles.

Paul, in fact, said, "I thank my God, I speak with tongues more than ye all," (14:18) — Greek, Aramaic, and the languages of the Romans, and the barbarian tribes. This may assume the miraculous gift of tongues since he probably could not have known all of these language-dialects by his own study in view of the time factor of the Acts. Compare Acts 2:8-11.

Recall Mark 16:20, "And they went forth, and preached everywhere, the Lord working with them, and confirming the Word with signs following. Amen." Today that need for speaking in tongues has ceased. God has authenticated these men and the New Testament penned by them. The temporary character of tongues is thus further supported.

Factors Relating to the Historical Cessation of The Gift of Tongues. We have referred briefly to the cessation of the gifts of prophecy, healing, and of apostleship. In other words, they were temporary gifts.

There was also the cessation of sudden judgments. In the early days of the church God dealt with sin among the believers and among the critics of the gospel by immediate physical judgments.

In 32 A.D. Ananias and Sapphira received the death penalty from God immediately for lying, (Acts 5:1-11). In 44 A.D. judgment was pronounced on Herod in a similar way, (Acts 12:20-25).

Later, however, in 60-70 A.D. God was not dealing with men in the same way. In 64 A.D., for example, Alexander, a blasphemer, was turned over to Satan by Paul, but three years later he still had not been judged, (I Tim. 1:19, 20). In 67 A.D. Alexander still was not punished for what he had done to Paul, (II Tim. 4:14-15).

Miraculous prison escapes also ceased. Early in the Acts both Peter and Paul experienced miraculous deliverances, (Acts 5:19-20; 16:25ff).

Later in the first century God's servants were no longer delivered from prison by a miracle. All of the apostles except John died a martyr's death.

All this suggests that miraculous gifts were passing from the church by the end of the apostolic era and constitutes further evidence that the gift of tongues is no longer in the church today.

"Therefore, as far as the leading Christian historians know, no parallel phenomenon to the New Testament gift of tongues has occurred. The outbreaks generally cited as parallel often led to heresy and fanaticism. So, we may conclude that the indications of Scripture fit the experience of history and combine to affirm that the gift of tongues passed from the church in the first century."[10]

Two of the best known and greatest of the early Church Fathers looked back on those years with corroboration of the temporary aspect of tongues.

Chrysostom (347-407 A.D.) commented on the I Corinthian passage: "This whole place is very obscure: but the obscurity is produced by our ignorance of the facts referred to and by their cessation, being such as then used to occur, but now no longer take place."[11]

Augustine (354-430 A.D.) said in speaking of Acts 2:4, "In the earliest times, 'the Holy Ghost fell upon them that believed: and they spake with tongues' . . . These were signs adapted to the time. For there behooved to be that betokening of the Holy Spirit . . .that thing was done for a betokening, and it passed away."[12]

Conclusion. The Word specifically states, "Whether there be tongues, they shall cease," (13:8). In summary, the five additional factors supporting the temporary aspect of tongues are:

1. **Relating to God's Covenant Relationship to Israel.** Tongues were a sign of judgment upon unbelieving Israel. When that judgment was completed, the need for the sign gift ceased.

2. **Relating to the Foundation Period of the Church.** Tongues were current in the infancy of the church, but ceased in its maturity.

3. **Relating to the Closing of the Canon.** When the New Testament was written, there was no longer any need for a confirming sign.

4. **Relating to the Authentication of Christ and the Apostles.** After authentication was finished and the New Testament was complete, there was no further need of speaking in tongues.

5. **Relating to the Historical Cessation of the Gift of Tongues.** As other gifts, miraculous judgments, and special deliverances disappeared, further supporting evidence develops that the miraculous gift of tongues was passing, too.

Since there is good biblical support that speaking in tongues was a temporary gift for the infant, immature New Testament church, it is concluded that speaking in tongues is not for today.

CHAPTER TEN

The Greater Gift
(Read I Corinthians 14:1-19)

In *A Handbook for Tongues, Interpretation and Prophecy*, Don Basham, a leading charismatic writer, includes a poem by Pastor Ernie Gruen[1] who says, "My prayer to God was like this:

'Lord, if I don't get what the apostles got
The way they got what they got,
Then I won't know that I got what they got.
But Lord, if I get what they got
The way they got what they got,
Then I'll know I got what they got.' "

Though spoken earnestly, this poem reflects several things.

Perhaps unintentionally, a suggestion of compulsion comes in lines 1 and 2. The attitude does not seem to be one of seeking God's will but rather, "Lord, You must grant this request."

How do we know that we have the baptism of the Holy Spirit? By experience or by the Word of God? Paul has already shared that all believers have been baptized into one body (I Cor. 12:13) and have been joined to Christ the head of that body, (Gal. 3:27). The continuing basic issue regarding tongues is, "Do I base my belief on experiences or upon the written, infallible Word of God?"

One more reflection on the poem above . . . If you were to speak in tongues, how would you know, really know, that you did not get something else besides what the apostles got?

Remember that I Corinthians 12 concerns *principles*. Chapter 13 relates the *spirit* of the ministry of the gifts to the superiority of love and of Christ. Strong evidence was given of the temporary aspect of the gift of tongues as the church moved from infancy to maturity.

Continuing in I Corinthians, chapter 14 looks to the *exercise* of the gift of tongues and to the regulation of that gift in the primitive, apostolic assembly of saints.

I. CONTRAST OF PURPOSE AND RESULT, vv. 1-4

Paul contrasts the purpose of speaking in tongues with prophesying and looks at the results. Verses 1-19 give reasons why the gift of prophecy is greater than the gift of tongues. By *interpretation* prophecy in this chapter refers to the primary sense of foretelling, but may be *applied* to the secondary sense of forthtelling today. The first word of verse 2, "for," suggests that reasons will follow for the greater gift of prophecy.

"Follow after charity, and desire spirituals, but rather that ye may prophesy," (v. 1). The key statement, "but rather that ye may prophesy," states a preference. We often say, "I would rather do *this* than *that*." Paul's goal in writing to the Corinthians was that they would *rather* prophesy than speak in tongues. What is our "rather"? Will the choice be for self-edification or church-edification?

Remember that this was in Paul's day when the gift was *still present though decreasing* and second, that Paul was dealing with the *abuse* of a *descending* gift, *not* the *use* of an *ascending* gift.[2]

The apostle now explains why prophecy is the greater gift. "For he that speaketh in an unknown tongue speaketh not unto men, but unto God: for no man understandeth him; howbeit in the Spirit he speaketh mysteries," (v. 2). (Remember to omit the italicized word *unknown* throughout this chapter.)

Verse 2 contrasts the Corinthians' use of tongues with God's desire. They were using tongues to their personal advantage. They were becoming wrapped up in their own abilities and selfish spiritual superiorities. Note the contrast of the phrase "unto God" in verse 2 and "unto men" in verse 3. Tongues-speaking was not understood by others. It involved mysteries, whereas the one who proclaimed the Word "speaketh unto men" with practical, genuine help.

The profit of the contrast appears in verse 3, "but he that prophesieth speaketh unto men to edification, and exhortation, and comfort." Prophecy profits the church. People will gain from edification ("to build up"), exhortation ("to stir up"), and comfort ("to cheer up"). In using tongues, an individual speaks to edify himself. But exercising prophecy edifies the church, (v. 4).

You may enjoy tongues, but no one else may. It is something like singing a solo. You sound great in the shower, splendid out in the woods or on a mountainside, but if you were to sing in a crowd, you might put someone else out of tune. You would enjoy it, but others might not! Similarly, if one speaks in tongues he edifies himself, but others are not edified.

The Corinthians were using tongues for personal advantage. Prophecy has wider benefits. Prophecy reaches many people with the blessings of the gospel and the ministry of edification, exhortation, and comfort. The believer needs to be sensitive to the contrast between the gifts of tongues and prophecy.

II. INTERPRETATION OF TONGUES, vv. 5-6

The interpretation of tongues enters the picture. "I would that ye all spake with tongues, but rather that ye prophesied: for greater is he that prophesieth than he that speaketh with tongues, except he interpret, that the church may receive edifying," (v. 5).

The words "but rather" appear again in this verse. Once more there is a choice. We are exercising the greater gift when we prophesy than when we speak in tongues.

Two problems develop. Does Paul's wish in verse 5 that they all spoke with tongues contradict this "rather" preference? No! Although he knew that not all believers were so gifted, his wish is in keeping with the sign-gift purpose of verses 21-22. Jews were still in Corinth. They still needed that judicial sign gift of their unbelief! But even then Paul prefers prophecy! "But rather"!

The second problem is found in the last part of verse 5. Does it infer that, if there is interpretation, tongues would be equal with prophecy? Yes, in one sense, but the very situation of tongues needing interpretation proves prophecy is a greater gift. The Greek word for "interpretation" is intensive, meaning a need for translation and full explanation.

Paul continues, "Now, brethren, if I come unto you speaking in tongues, what shall I profit you, except I shall speak to you either by revelation, or by knowledge, or by prophesying, or by doctrine?" (v. 6). He asks what profit would come to the church if he should speak in tongues without interpretation. Would revelation, knowledge, prophecy, or doctrine be understood and benefit his listeners? The answer is "no"!

Tongues is an inferior method of communicating truth to the church because an interpreter is needed. Prophecy needs no interpreter!

The principle is: *communication resulting in understanding is profitable!*

III. COMMUNICATION WITH PROFIT, vv. 7-12

In verses 7-12 Paul presents a series of illustrations to

demonstrate his further reasons why prophecy is greater than tongues.

He illustrates his point using musical instruments. "And even things without life-giving sound, whether pipe or harp, except they give a distinction in the sounds, how shall it be known what is piped or harped? For if the trumpet give an uncertain sound, who shall prepare himself to the battle? So likewise ye, except ye utter by the tongue words easy to be understood, how shall it be known what is spoken? For ye shall speak into the air," (vv. 7-9).

The trumpet call for battle in verse 8 refers to the special Jewish call to arms using the silver trumpets. Numbers 10:1-10 describes six different uses of two silver trumpets. The people received Moses' directions through the distinct trumpet sounds during their marches toward Canaan.

Israel had a special alarm for war. "And if ye go to war in your land against the enemy that oppresseth you, then ye shall blow an alarm with the trumpet; and ye shall be remembered before the Lord your God, and ye shall be saved from your enemies," (Numb. 10:9). If Israel could not distinguish between these trumpet calls, would they prepare for battle? (v. 8).

Verse 9 applies the trumpet illustration. "So likewise ye". Unless we speak easily understood words, how will people know what is being said? It will be like speaking into the air. Communication without understanding is unprofitable. Communication with understanding is profitable.

The illustrations continue with kinds of voices or languages in verses 10 and 11.

"There are, it may be, so many kinds of voices in the world, and none of them is without signification. Therefore, if I know not the meaning of the voice, I shall be unto him that speaketh a barbarian, and he that speaketh shall be a barbarian unto me."

Scholars have counted about 5000 spoken languages in the world, plus dialects which are local forms of a language. Some of these languages and dialects are spoken only by small groups of a few hundred or a few thousand persons. But whether Chinese, Russian, Waiwai, or Nepalese, each is significant. If one listens and cannot understand the language-voice, what profit is there for either the speaker or the listener?

These illustrations of music and language underline the principle before us: communication without understanding is not profitable. If speaking in tongues does not bring understanding, it is not profitable. Even when interpreted, it is less desirable. Prophecy is the greater gift.

The great goal reappears in verse 12. "Even so ye, forasmuch as ye are zealous of spiritual gifts, seek that ye may excel to the edifying of the church." Edifying the church is the great goal. Prophecy and communication with understanding will achieve this goal.

IV. PRAYING IN TONGUES, vv. 13-17

In the primitive church, the Corinthians were to pray for interpretation of tongues to communicate with understanding and thus edify the church. "Wherefore let him that speaketh in a tongue pray that he may interpret," (v. 13).

Paul spoke of self-edification by tongues in verse 4. He presented this as inferior to prophecy or "the presentation of new revelations from God," by foretelling.

Now he speaks of one channel of self-edification by tongues — perhaps the most important channel. He strikes at the heart of the Corinthian situation and also of those today who look to tongues self-edification. An important question arises. Is it scriptural to pray in tongues in order to receive personal edification?

"For if I pray in a tongue, my spirit prayeth, but my understanding is unfruitful. What is it then? I will pray with the spirit, and I will pray with the understanding also: I will sing with the spirit, and I will sing with the understanding also," (vv. 14-15).

Did Paul encourage private praying in tongues? No! Paul says in verse 15 that he prayed with both his understanding and the Spirit's blessing at the same time. The "understanding" and the "Spirit" are not separated; they are joined.

When Paul prayed, he understood what he was saying. His whole personality was involved. This he contrasted as superior to praying in a tongue.

In the goddess Diana worship, the heathen prayed in ecstatic speech without engaging their minds or understanding. The Corinthians were using the then-legitimate gift of tongues the way they used ecstatic speech in their pagan worship before becoming Christians. Paul rejects this.

Jesus had previously warned against improper prayer. In Matt. 6:7 He said, "Use not vain repetitions, as the heathen do." The heathen refers to Gentiles with whom ecstatic prayer was common. The term rendered "vain repetitions" comes from the Greek verb *battalogeo* which means "to repeat idly" or "to speak batta, batta, batta".

Dr. Carl Pfeil, author of *Charismatic Concerns*, states "'batta' is a peculiar Greek term which pictured by its sound just what it meant — nonsensical, meaningless sounds. So in this very important statement of prohibition, our Savior forbids us to pray with sounds which we don't ourselves understand, like the Gentiles who in their pagan temples prayed daily with ecstatic — but meaningless — sounds."[3]

Instead Christ said, "Pray like this," and He gave the model Lord's prayer with every word and phrase entirely meaningful to the speaker.

Some tongues advocates have tried to find praying in tongues in Romans 8:26, which says, "Likewise the Spirit also helpeth our infirmities: for we know not what we should pray for as we ought: but the Spirit Himself maketh intercession for us with groanings which cannot be uttered."

Look closely. Speaking in tongues is not in this verse. You will note the "groanings" are *not utterable!*

Whether praying in the Spirit, singing in the Spirit, or blessing in the Spirit, Paul states he will do all with understanding that there may be edification of others, vv. 16-17.

V. A NUMERICAL COMPARISON, vv. 18-19

Paul now makes a confession. "I thank my God, I speak with tongues more than you all," (v. 18).

We have already noted the fact that in his many travels, Paul spoke with the tongues of the Greeks, the Romans, the barbarians as well as Aramaic, and that "more than ye all."

Remember in addition that Paul is an apostle, that Israel is still in the land, and that the judicial sign judgment has not yet fallen. Therefore, Paul is still in the position of warning unbelieving Israel personally, through the use of the sign gift of tongues!

In his confession Paul makes a very important comparison. "Yet in the church I had rather speak five words with my understanding, that by my voice I might teach others also, than ten thousand words in a tongue," (v. 19). Tongues are here said to consist of words which carry meaning, not ecstatic utterances of foolish gibberish.

The rate of preference of understandable speech to such tongues is staggering — 5 words of speech to 10,000 words in tongues. The ratio here is 2000 to 1! Gardiner points out that 10,000 was the highest number the Greeks had, so the comparison could be paraphrased in our day as "a million to five!"[4]

Unfortunately today some would reverse the ratio and would rather speak 10,000 words in a tongue and only 5 words with understanding.

Notice again the word "rather" in verse 19. This is the third such reference of preference in this chapter.

In summary, prophecy is greater than tongues because:

1. Its purpose is greater — for edification, exhortation, and comfort.

2. Tongues tend to self-edification, prophecy to church edification.

3. Tongues need an interpreter; prophecy needs no interpreter.

4. Tongues, in themselves, are not understood and therefore not profitable. Prophecy can be understood and is profitable. Communication with understanding is profitable whether to God or to men.

5. Looking ahead in the chapter, tongues brought ridicule (v. 23), prophecy brought conviction to the sinner unto salvation and worship of God (vv. 24-25).

As Dillow summarizes, prophecy is superior to or greater than tongues in communication, vv. 1-12, in praise, vv. 13-19, and in evangelism, vv. 20-25.[5]

Paul stated that he would rather speak five words with his understanding. What might those five words be? He told the Corinthians in the resurrection chapter that "Christ died for our sins." That was the message then and it is still the message for today. Declare it faithfully!

CHAPTER ELEVEN

Purpose and Order
(Read I Corinthians 14:20-40)

From Paul's proof of prophecy as the greater gift, he turns to the purpose and order of the lesser gift, of speaking in tongues. The genuine gift of speaking in tongues was still present in the Corinthian assembly, but that church had been very hazy concerning the true purpose of this gift. Confusion had arisen concerning the proper and spiritual order of its usage.

Before Paul attempts to lift the mind and heart of the Corinthians to the theme of the Lord Jesus Christ's coming and the first resurrection in chapter 15, he sharpens their appreciation of the real purpose of speaking in tongues. He explains the precise order in which tongues were to be used. His first emphasis is purpose.

I. PURPOSE OF THE GIFT, vv. 20-22

Verse 20 appeals to Christians — brethren. It summarizes the preceding portion of the chapter in its basic premise that prophecy is the greater gift. "Brethren, be not children in understanding: howbeit in malice be ye children, but in understanding be men!"

With prophecy comes understanding and maturity. The thought is to continue to be innocent babes in matters of evil but in understanding be mature as men. One strong indication of maturity is to acknowledge the authority of God's Word over experience. The Word provides the true basis and motivation for wonderful and practical experiences in life.

The key purpose of tongues is presented in verses 21 and 22. "In the law it is written, with men of other tongues and other lips will I speak unto this people: and yet for all that will they not hear me, saith the Lord. Wherefore tongues are for a sign, not to them that believe, but to them that believe not: but prophesying serveth not for them that believe not, but for them which believe." One of the five reasons for the temporary character of the gift of tongues is this key purpose concerning God's covenant relationship to Israel. Tongues were a sign gift in judgment upon unbelieving Israel.

Verse 21 refers particularly to Isaiah 28:11-12 and the time of judgment upon Israel during the Assyrian captivity in 721 B.C. The Jews heard the Assyrian tongue at that time. In application, for more than 1900 years this condition has been largely true as Gentiles of different tongues have witnessed the gospel to the Jews who, with predicted national blindness of unbelief, have rejected it.

Tongues were the judicial sign from God of Jewish confirmed unbelief. When the judgment was completed, the need for this key purpose ceased.

Remember that tongues were a sign *not for the believer*, but *for the unbelieving Jew*. "Wherefore tongues are for a sign . . . to them that believe not." As Zane C. Hodges notes, the conclusive word *wherefore* suggests that the statement to follow is the result of a legitimate deduction from the Old Testament Scripture just presented in which the apostle discovered the true intent of this miraculous phenomenon.

"The use of the definite article with the Greek word for 'tongues' (*ai glossai*) (the tongues) . . . further confirms that Paul finds this particular phenomenon to be the thing referred to by the Scripture he has cited."[1] "Wherefore, *the* tongues are for a sign."

Furthermore tongues were not merely *a* sign. The word translated "for" is the Greek preposition *eis* which here indicates purpose. Thus Paul is stating that not only are tongues *a* sign, but that they were intended to be such. "Tongues are *for* a sign."

God was responding to something that was peculiarly Jewish, the desire for signs. "For the Jews require a sign," (I Cor. 1:22). Many other verses support this, such as Matthew 12:38; 16:1-4; and John 6:30.

On the other hand, prophecy is especially for believers. "But prophesying serveth not for them that believe not, but for them which believe," (v. 22b).

From this key purpose Paul now turns to order in the local church.

II. ORDER OF THE USE OF THE GIFT, vv. 23-40

Setting. We are looking at the Corinthian Church in Paul's day where the gift of tongues was being abused by the believers. Paul was writing concerning the exercise of that gift when the gift was decreasing in accord with its temporary character.

The references to the church are significant in this passage. "The whole church be come together in one place," (v. 23), "there come in," twice used in verses 23-24 and implying a local assembly, "brethren, when ye come together," (v. 26), "in the church," (v. 28), "as in all churches of the saints," (v. 33), "in the churches," (v. 34), and the contrast of "at home" and "in the church," (v. 35). This list of church references clarifies the fact that in this passage the order for exercising the gift of tongues refers to usage *in the local church.*

Tongues or prophecy, vv. 23-25. Paul has already taught that prophecy is the greater gift together with the reasons for this conclusion in verses 1-19. He continues this argument in verses 23-25.

"If therefore the whole church be come together into one place, and all speak with tongues, and there come in those that are unlearned, or unbelievers, will they not say that ye are mad? But if all prophesy, and there come in one that believeth not, or one unlearned, he is convinced of all, he is judged of all: and thus are the secrets of his heart made manifest; and so falling down on his face he will worship God, and report that God is in you of a truth," (vv. 23-25).

Two situations are before us in these verses where uninitiated believers and unbelievers enter the church and sit down. One of two things happens. Either "all (believers) speak in tongues," (v. 23), or "all (believers) prophesy," (v. 24).

If "all speak in tongues," v. 23, the result is ridicule from the uninitiated believers or the unbelievers who enter the church and listen. They receive no profit. Remember that "communication without understanding is unprofitable."

However, "if all prophesy," v. 24, in an orderly and understandable way, conviction of sin results. The uninitiated believer or unbeliever humbles himself before God in worship. The result is reality, not ridicule. Again our principle is illustrated, "communication with understanding is profitable!"

Therefore, the order for the local church was a communicating prophecy.

Liberty for ministry of the gifts, v. 26. The early saints had liberty in Christ in ministering and exercising their gifts in the assembly, but this led to confusion. Everyone had a psalm, a doctrine, a tongue, a revelation, an interpretation.

"How is it then, brethren? When ye come together everyone of you hath a psalm, hath a doctrine, hath a tongue, hath a revelation, hath an interpretation. Let all things be done unto edifying," (v. 26).

Paul's exhortation, "Let all things be done to edifying," is the first of two "let all things . . ." admonitions in this chapter. Verse 40 gives the other, "Let all things be done decently and in order." These appeals dovetail. If there is going to be any edification, there must be decency and order.

One other similar admonition occurs in this letter near its conclusion. "Let all your things be done with clarity," (16:14). Paul's plea was for edification, decency and order, but most of all for love!

Rules for control of tongues in the early church, vv. 27-28. Paul lays out specific rules for controlling speaking in tongues. "If any man speak in a tongue, let it be by two, or at the most by three, and that by course; and let one interpret. But if there be no interpreter, let him keep silence in the church; and let him speak to himself, and to God," (vv. 27-28). *First*, no more than three were to speak in tongues at one occasion, v. 27a. "Let it be by two, or at the most by three." *Second*, these must speak in turn or "by course," v. 27b. *Third*, if there was no interpreter, the one speaking in tongues must be silent. Paul intimates that this interpretation is limited to only one person. "And let one interpret. But if there be no interpreter, let him keep silence in the church," (vv. 27b-28a).

Please note that it is not certain that Paul is referring to speaking in tongues when he mentions speaking to oneself and to God in verse 28. In view of Paul's earlier injunction that prayer without an interpreter causes the mind to be unfruitful, (14:14), it seems unlikely that he now would approve of a means of prayer that he considered to be unprofitable. If one takes the opposite view, one would conclude that prayer to God in tongues would be by permission and not by recommendation.[2]

A *fourth rule* for controlling tongues relates to purpose and to tongues' use. Tongues must be exercised for the edification or building up of the saints. "Let all things be done unto edifying," v. 26b. The gift also must be discharged "decently and in order," v. 40. "For God is not the author of confusion, but of peace, as in all churches of the saints," (v. 33).

Rules for control of prophecy in the early church, vv. 29-33. These verses concern the primary meaning of the prophet as the revealer of new truth from God. Until the New Testament was written, new revelations suiting the new dispensation of grace were given through prophecy.

Two or three prophets spoke and the others (pl.) were to judge, v. 29. Part of the standard of that judgment was disclosed in I Corinthians 12:3 whether or not the lordship of Christ were acknowledged. This prophetic gift was to be orderly with only one speaking at a time, verse 30. "If anything be revealed to another that sitteth by, let the first hold his peace." "One by one" is the clear direction of verse 31. "For ye may all prophesy one by one, that all may learn, and all may be comforted."

Again we see that prophecy was valued as more acceptable than tongues. Only three "at the most" could speak in tongues, (v. 27), but *all* could prophesy as the Spirit led.

A basic principle for prophecy, tongues and the other gifts is highlighted in verse 32. "And the spirits of the prophets are subject to the prophets." This does not mean that the spirit of a prophet speaking is to be subject to another prophet seated nearby. Rather this means that the spirit of the prophet speaking is to be subject to himself. *At no time is he to lose control.* Nor is the tongues-speaker to lose control, as verse 28 unfolds. Where no interpreter stood at hand, he was to control the power and be silent in the church.

Verse 33 provides a summary for controlling speaking in tongues and speaking in prophecy. The verse says that God is not the author of confusion but of peace.

The Greek word used here for confusion (*akatastasia*) is rare in the New Testament. Its basic thought is instability. God doesn't cause instability. Instability leads to confusion.[3]

Here is an important alternative. Do we want confusion in the church or do we want peace? If confusion is present, that confusion is not from God. But real peace comes from God!

The Scripture has revealed four rules for controlling

speaking in tongues in the church. Next, a *fifth rule* comes to light.

Women with reference to tongues and prophecy, vv. 34-35. Whole books have been written on these verses. "Let your women keep silence in the churches: for it is not permitted unto them to speak; but they are commanded to be under obedience, as also saith the law. And if they will learn anything, let them ask their husbands at home: for it is a shame for women to speak in the church," (vv. 34-35).

The Word does not specifically state whether this appeal to women concerns tongues or prophecy. But because speech is required for both tongues and prophecy, it can be concluded that this controlling regulation is set forth for both. The eight occurrences of "speak" in vv. 21-40 support this.

This direction for women comes near the end of chapters 12-14, also near the end of the regulations for exercising the gift of tongues. In the overall content of Paul's message to the Corinthian Church, the Holy Spirit's placement of this exhortation may be significant.

Paul gives two regulations to women — to keep silent in the church and to obey or be in submission.

How far women's silence goes varies greatly in local churches. Surely it refers to tongues and prophecy in its primary form, and usually to forthtelling or preaching in its secondary form.

If this one regulation of the early church were heeded today in charismatic circles, about 70-80% of present glossolalia would cease. If more regulations were heeded, an even greater percentage would cease.

With good insight Gardiner points out that because of the Jewish attitude toward women and, in particular, because of many Greek Aphrodite prostitute priestesses present at Corinth, the Jews would not receive God's judgment sign gift of tongues through women in the churches. Thus the effectiveness of the judicial sign of judgment would be utterly lost to that people.[4]

Paul stated that women should never usurp the authority God gave to the men to lead in the public life of the church, (I Tim. 2:11-12). This may be applied to tongues-speaking today.

Women are "to subject themselves (imperative middle) or obey just as the law says," v. 34b, i.e. as quoted from the law, located in the first five books of the Bible. One such quotation could be Genesis 3:16b: "And thy desire shall be to thy husband, and he shall rule over thee."

Equality of spiritual privilege of men and women before God does not nullify the principle of subordination or headship in the church. God ordained this and it has not changed.[5]

If women needed clarification concerning doctrine or messages, they were to ask their husbands about the matter at home in the early church.

Conclusion, vv. 36-40. The question of verse 36, "What? Came the Word of God out from you? Or came it unto you only?" points out again that individuals are not to decide what they are going to accept or reject. The authority of the Bible is to be champion over experience and human reasoning. God speaks with authority. His people are to do as He commands.

"If any man think himself to be a prophet, or spiritual, let him acknowledge that the things that I write unto you are the commandments of the Lord," (v. 37). Paul is speaking of the commandments of the Lord in the previous passage concerning the order in the local assembly, especially respecting tongues. Any Corinthian who thought he was spiritual was to note that these things are the commandments of the Lord.

Any man objecting to this Paul places among those who are ill-taught. "But if any man be ignorant, let him be ignorant," (v. 38). Grammatically, "Let him be ignorant" is in the middle voice. Paul is saying, "Let him take the consequences himself of his ignorance, not pretending to be wiser than those who obey the commandments of the Lord."

The "wherefore" of verse 39 introduces the final conclusion of this major tongues passage. "Wherefore, brethren, covet to prophesy, and forbid not to speak with tongues," (v. 39). "Eagerly desire" to prophesy or foretell, not to speak in tongues. This exhortation to the whole asssembly of believers encouraged them to covet the ministry of men prophesying in their midst and to share in this gift themselves as God had sovereignly bestowed it upon them.[6]

But what did Paul mean when he said, "Forbid not to speak with tongues," verse 39? Exactly what he said. Do not forbid anyone from speaking in tongues if he or she meets all the proper regulations, though Paul was not encouraging speaking in tongues. Israel was still in the land. God had not yet sent the judgment. Therefore the warning was still going forth through the sign gift, which had not yet ceased.

If I were in Paul's sandals in Paul's day, speaking to the primitive assembly still possessing the gift of tongues, this would be a right and proper admonition. But I am not in Paul's sandals, not in his day, nor in the primitive assembly. Rather I live in a day in which the teaching of the Word favors cessation of tongues. Furthermore, God has sent his dispersing judgment upon Israel. Therefore, this exhortation would not be proper today.

Finally, Paul says, "Let all things be done decently," meaning "respectably," and "in order," (v. 40). All things are to be done by "arrangement," such as the Word of God authorizes, not substituting an order which it condemns.

It is never right for finite man to limit the infinite God at any time. In His sovereignty and power He is able to allow the genuine gift of speaking in tongues to be transacted today. But in light of history and of the direct teaching of the Word of God, it is unlikely that He often does this. God moves and works according to the authority and statement of His Word.

CHAPTER TWELVE

The Contemporary Scene

As mentioned earlier, many Christians today are experiencing something which they call tongues. I have heard their testimonies in part and read of them, and I do not question the genuineness of these experiences. The issue is not, are they genuine, but are they scriptural?

The previous chapters sought to clarify the scriptural teaching through expositional studies of Acts, I Corinthians and other passages. I trust we agree that the authority of Scripture is greater than the authority of experience. But what is the meaning of the contemporary scene?

I. THE CONDITION AND THE CAUSE

People from all denominations and faiths are speaking in tongues. Adherents include people from all social strata and ethnic backgrounds. Some even believe that the charismatic movement forms the third force in Christendom today — Catholicism, Protestantism, and Pentecostalism.[1]

Even more important, it appears that a strategic mechanism is unfolding before our eyes to facilitate the formation of the prophetic world church of end times. While Christian and non-Christian groups would never unite on the basis of doctrine, they can and will unite if they sacrifice doctrine in favor of experience. Current evidence presents tongues as one of the factors of that unifying experience.

The basic cause for the charismatic movement has been a lack of knowledge concerning the Word of God and the appropriation of that Word in people's daily experiences. Nature abhors a vacuum, whether physical or spiritual. The phenomena of glossolalia has rushed to fill that vacuum.

Gardiner sees four groups besides the traditional Pentecostals of which this is true:[2]

Liberal churches where people have been receiving "stones" for "bread" wanted something more than social action and human philosophy. A so-called spiritual, respectable experience appealed to these thirsty, hungry people.

Roman Catholic charismatics who still remain loyal to the church and its dogmas found glossolalia a welcome contrast to sacramentalism and the mass.

Orthodox churches where the Bible has been believed, but the preaching has been too dry, dull, intellectual and impractical — removed from life — have turned to tongues.

Youth turned off by ritualistic churches, disillusioned by drugs, the occult, and free sex found tongues to be a new and different "high".

If the Scripture had been taught with relevance and the Bible had been obeyed, there would be no need of so-called spiritual fulfillment in glossolalia.

What is the source of today's speaking in tongues?

II. ANALYSIS

Some speaking in tongues may be satanic. As indicated earlier in the historical sketch, many authorities point out that glossolalia does occur outside the realm of Christianity.

"Edward Langston says that in East Africa many

persons possessed by demons speak fluently in Swahili or English, although under normal circumstances they do not understand either language."[3]

Today ecstatic speech is found among the Moslems and also the Eskimos of Greenland. The Bwiti cult among the Fang people of the Gabon Republic has been observed speaking in tongues. Mormons claim to speak in tongues, as do the Jehovah's Witnesses.[4]

It is interesting that the modern charismatic movement often includes those who do not meet the biblical standards to be "born again" believers. The Holy Spirit does not indwell an unbeliever. Yet these people speak in tongues. Could this "spirit" be another? The possibility of satanic influence, therefore, cannot be brushed aside. Just because we hear an unusual ecstatic utterance or even genuine speaking in foreign languages doesn't prove that the glossolalia is of God.

More speaking in tongues is psychological. There are several ways in which it is induced.[5]

Some of it is caused by *ecstacy.* In a highly emotional state, the person is out of his ordinary frame of mind, and pours forth impassioned utterances.

Another possible cause is *auto-hypnosis* (self-hypnosis). In cases of auto-hypnosis, there is almost always a sense of frustration and inner conflict, especially with Christians who feel dissatisfied with their experience and are searching for the "secret" of the abundant life. Tongues promises to be an end to the tension and people subconsciously begin to seek it.

Or the gift may be presented as *the acme of Christian experience* and the hallmark of spiritual prestige. Tongues may be accompanied by feelings of group acceptance and divine approval.

"Hypnotizability" has been called an essential of most experiences of glossolalia, even the *sina qua non* of tongues-speaking.[6] Whether naturally submissive and dependent on a leader or not, people yield to the power of suggestion and do whatever is being suggested.

Another way to describe either hypnosis or auto-hypnosis is giving up control of thought and speech patterns by consciously yielding to "outside" influences in a passive way or "letting yourself go". The would-be tongues speaker need only say a few words, letting them flow without thinking about what he is saying.

Dr. E. Mansell Pattison of the University of Washington School of Medicine, and a member of the Christian Association for Psychological Studies, states, "In certain types of brain disorders resulting from strokes, brain tumors, etc., the patient is left with disruptions in his automatic physical speech circuit patterns. If we study these 'aphasic' patients, we can observe the same decomposition of speech that occurs in glossolalia." Dr. Pattison thus compares the results of some brain injuries on speech to the results of renouncing control by some tongues speakers.[7]

Remember, if we let ourselves go, we are disobeying the Word of God. "And the spirits of the prophets are subject to the prophets," (I Cor. 14:32). God never leads His children into loss of control. That action was typical of the paganism out of which the Corinthians had come. They had been carried away or swept away unto idols, (I Cor. 12:2).

Satan is always ready to take advantage of an "out-of-control" situation with regrettable results: there can be psychological damage to the individual. Gardiner says that "Charismatic writers are constantly warning tongues-speakers that they will suffer a let-down."[8] The true gift of tongues in Acts knows no let-down.

Speaking in tongues may be a learned behaviour, as well as satanic or psychological. John F. MacArthur in his book *The Charismatics* states that this may be the *most common explanation* for the tongues that are occurring in the charismatic movement today.[9] His analysis suggests that tongues-speaking is not a super-natural experience nor a miracle but that a person learns how to do it.

John Kildahl, a clinical psychologist, and his partner Paul Qualben, a psychiatrist, were commissioned by the American Lutheran Church and the National Institute of Mental Health to do a long-range study on tongues.

In his book *The Psychology of Speaking in Tongues*, Kildahl defines tongues as a definitely learned skill. With his partner Qualben, Kildahl came to the firm conviction that it was nothing more than learned behavior.[10]

Why a person has to "learn" to receive a "gift" from the Holy Spirit is unexplainable, but teaching how to speak in tongues goes on continuously in the charismatic movement.

Gardiner says, ". . . ecstatic experience, like drug-addiction, requires larger and larger doses to satisfy. Sometimes the bizarre is introduced. I have seen people run around a room until they were exhausted, climb tent poles, laugh hysterically, go into trances for days and do other weird things as the "high" sought became more elusive.

Eventually there is a crisis and a decision is made; he will sit on the back seats and be a spectator, "fake it," go on in the hope that everything will eventually be as it was. The most tragic decision is to quit and in the quitting abandon all things spiritual as fraudulent. The spectators are frustrated, the fakers suffer guilt, the hoping are pitiable and the quitters are a tragedy. No, such movements are not harmless!"[11]

But is all speaking in tongues satanic, psychological or learned? How does one account for genuine examples of foreign language in glossolalia today? At least 73% of the tongues-speakers today believe that they are speaking in a language.[12] Some possible answers are:[13]

First, sometimes the objectivity of the report may be questioned, the language claims being based on non-specialists rather than linguists.

Second, often the reports of languages turn out to be only a few words and not a fluent language.

Third, cryptomnesia, the appearance in the conscious mind of what was once stored in the memory and then forgotten could explain the languages. Stress causes the so-called hidden language to be released in a language never "learned" but which may have been overheard, such as two foreigners talking, or expressions from some other source forgotten to the person's conscious mind.

Donald W. Burdick concludes that present-day glossolalia is not foreign-language speaking because of the following reasons:[14]

1. The high frequency of repetition in tongues-speaking. Similar-sounding syllables are repeated over and over.

2. The similarity of tongues speech to the speaker's own language background.

3. The excessive use of one or two vowels.

4. The absence of any language structure.

5. The markedly greater length of the interpretation as compared with the tongues utterance.

6. The inconsistency of the interpretation of the same phrase or clause.

7. The predominately King James style employed in interpretation. Does God speak in 17th century English?

Burdick,[15] Smith,[16] and others have noted that such men as Dr. Kenneth Pike, the famous linguist of the University of Michigan, and Eugene Nida, the renowned linguist with the American Bible Society, assisted by many specialists, find that tongues bear no resemblance to any actual language ever treated by linguistics.

These factors help us to see through the apparent foreign language clauses.

III. SUMMARY

The command of I Corinthians 14:39b, "forbid not to

speak in tongues," is not in order today because we are not in Paul's sandals in Paul's day in the primitive assembly still possessing the gift of tongues. But what if we were? It would be important to apply the ten tests for valid tongues-speaking as suggested by Dillow.[17]

1. It must be a foreign language spoken on earth, (Acts 2).

2. It must be used as a judicial sign to unbelieving Jews, (I Cor. 14:21-22).

3. It must be used publicly, and not privately, in accordance with its basic sign purpose and for edifying the church, (I Cor. 13:1; 14:12, 22).

4. It must be accompanied with a translation, (I Cor. 14:28).

5. It must be limited to three instances of tongues at any one service, (I Cor. 14:27).

6. It must be done one at a time, (I Cor. 14:27).

7. It must be limited to one interpretation, (I Cor. 14:27).

8. It must be exercised only by men in the church, (I Cor. 14:34).

9. It must be in balanced distribution with the other gifts, (I Cor. 12:17, 19).

10. It must be exercised in love, (I Cor. 13).

ALL ten of these criteria must be present at the same time to allow *scriptural tongues-speaking* today. Do you know anyone who has met *all* these criteria? If he does not meet these tests, then Paul would have forbidden him to speak in tongues, and Christians today should, too!

The tongues movement does result in harmful consequences. They are:[18]

1. Living by experience rather than the Word — living by "feelings rather than faith". A personal experience can easily substitute clear guidance from Scripture or serious Bible study.

2. Divisions among the churches. This division is based upon the doctrinal aberrations already cited and follows in the wake of the tongues movement.

3. A poor testimony to those who do not know Christ. Many are offended by the emotional excesses of the charismatic movement and turn away from salvation in Christ.

4. A fostering of pride. The individual who is able to speak in tongues may sense achievement and become proud of himself.

5. A merger of Christianity with paganism. Just as the tongues-speaking of the Corinthian Church paralleled their involvement in the Greek mystery religions prior to becoming Christians, there are striking similarities between the tongues movement and the practice of pagan tribes all over the world.

6. Superstition. Tongues-speaking is only one step away from the experience of "visions and direct revelations from God" which could even lead to disobeying constituted law and authority because "the Lord had told you".

But perhaps the greatest tragedy of the contemporary scene is the missing of the true Spirit-filled life.

Remember the dog in the ancient fable who, while crossing a bridge with a bone in his mouth, saw his reflection in the water below? The reflected bone looked so much better than the one in his mouth that he dropped the *substance for the shadow* and went hungry.

Many are like that dog today, ignoring the satisfying reality of the Spirit's fulness for a *shadow of an exciting experience* built around ecstatic speech.

Paul said, "And be not drunk with wine wherein is excess; but be filled with the Spirit," (Eph. 5:18). What does this filling mean?

Filling means "speaking to yourselves in psalms and hymns and spiritual songs, singing and making melody in your heart to the Lord; giving thanks always for all things unto God and the Father in the name of our Lord Jesus Christ," (Eph. 5:19-20). It means "submitting yourselves one to another in the fear of God," (v. 21).

"Wives (are to) submit themselves unto their own husbands, as unto the Lord," (v. 22). "Husbands (are to) love their wives even as Christ loved the church, and gave Himself for it," (v. 25). "Children (are to) obey their parents in the Lord," (Eph. 6:1). "Servants (are to) be obedient to their masters," (v. 5). Masters are to give due consideration to their servants, (v. 9).

The Spirit-filled person will also "be strong in the Lord, and in the power of His might," (v. 10).

He is to put on the whole armour of God "for we wrestle not against flesh and blood, but against principalities, against powers, against the rulers of the darkness of this world, against spiritual wickedness in high places," (v. 12).

Truth, righteousness, faith, salvation, the Word of God, and prayer are to be uppermost in the Spirit-filled Christian.

At the conclusion of his Ephesian letter, Paul asked the Christians to pray "for me, that *utterance may be given unto me* that I may *open my mouth boldly* to make known the mystery of the gospel, for which I am an ambassador in bonds: that therein I may *speak boldly*, as I ought to speak," (Eph. 6:19-20). May that be our prayer today.

CHAPTER THIRTEEN

Conclusion

The evidence points to one conclusion. Speaking in tongues was a temporary gift of the Holy Spirit for the early church and is not for today. The Biblical signals are clear. History supports the Word.

Historic glossolalia reveals that both Christians and non-Christians alike have spoken and do speak something they call tongues. To base the present-day tongues movement on the witness of church history would be inappropriate.

The New Testament gift of tongues began at Pentecost and enabled people to speak in real languages. Tongues are not the evidence of the baptism of the Holy Spirit today. The baptism of the Spirit is a sovereign positional work at the moment of salvation. Moral rather than miraculous confirmation should appear. At Pentecost tongues provided evidence of the Holy Spirit's residential coming into the world and authenticated the apostles and their message.

Tongues-speaking at Caesarea and Ephesus contributed evidence to Jewish Christians that Gentile believers also belonged to the body of Christ, the true Church. Once demonstrated in this transition from the dispensation of law to the dispensation of grace, there was no further need of such evidence to Jewish believers.

The Corinthian Church was not a spiritual church in spite of its glorious spiritual position in Christ. Rather, it was characterized by division, selfishness, criticism, toleration of evil, and immaturity. It manifested the gifts of the Spirit but not spiritual maturity.

Spiritual maturity is not determined by either the

possession or experience of spiritual gifts but rather by the growth which the Holy Spirit produces in the believer. The Corinthian Church failed to demonstrate growth in spite of their apparent emphasis on speaking in tongues.

The gifts are sovereignly bestowed by God as He desires, not as we want, and in amazing diversity in unity.

Looking at the many members of the physical body illustrates the truth of the many members of the spiritual body which are to operate without jealousy and imbalance, recognizing Christ as the head. Mutual care and respect prevent division of that body.

Paul sought to show the Corinthian Church that it has been seeking the lesser — tongues — instead of that which was more beneficial and greater — prophecy (fore-telling). He urged them to desire the greater gift for the edification of the church rather than the lesser gift of tongues for personal edification. Tongues also ranked last in the order of the importance of the gifts.

The Lord appropriately placed I Corinthians 13 at the heart of the major New Testament passage on tongues! The very spirit of the experience of this gift must be love, revealing that the truly spiritual life must be a life controlled by the Spirit of God as *evidenced by the fruit* of the Spirit, *not the gifts* of the Spirit. Speaking in tongues is worthless without love.

Besides the familiar promise "whether there be tongues, they shall cease," (I Cor. 13:8), five lines of evidence were brought forward to support the temporary aspect of the gift of tongues. Since this gift was temporary, speaking in tongues is not a biblical directive today.

I Corinthians 14 emphasizes the superiority of the prophecy gift over the tongues gift, urging the Corinthians to claim the greater, more beneficial gift rather than the lesser, more showy gift. A principle presented is that communication with understanding (prophecy) is profitable but that communication without understanding (tongues) is unprofitable. Paul was dealing with the abuse of a descending gift rather than the use of an ascending gift.

The basic purpose of tongues was to be the *judicial sign against Jewish unbelief as a nation.* A great deal hinges on this factor — that tongues were a sign *not for* the believer, but *for the unbelieving Jew.* When God's judgment on Jewish unbelief was completed, *the need for this key purpose closed.* The judgment of final dispersement may be dated at 70 A.D., when Jerusalem was destroyed by Roman armies.

The rules for speaking in tongues in the early church included the need for interpretation, edification, control, and its exercise by men alone.

Finally, the basic cause of present-day tongues-speaking has been a lack of the knowledge of the Word of God and its appropriation into daily life.

Phenomena of the present may be explained as either satanic, psychological — by ecstacy, self-hypnosis, or interference with the conscious control of the brain — or learned behaviors. Apparent foreign language manifestations are often inconsistent with fluent languages.

When scriptural tests are applied to possible tongues-speaking, it would appear very difficult to meet these criteria today.

In addition, harmful consequences from the tongues movement occur, the greatest tragedy of which is missing the true Spirit-filled life. When we have Christ, we already have everything, but we must claim our inheritance in Him!

One final appeal — heed the Scripture and love one another! Whether we speak in tongues or do not speak in tongues, we are to love one another as fellow-believers and to love a lost and dying world for whom Christ died.

We each possess a tongue — a gift from Him! Out of a heart in love with Jesus Christ may we each praise Him with that one tongue!

Notes

CHAPTER ONE

[1]James B. Pritchard, *Ancient Near Eastern Texts*, Vol. I, p. 26.

[2]Charles R. Smith, *Tongues In Biblical Perspective*, p. 15, as summarized from Plato's "Ion," "Apology," and "Timaeus".

[3]Virgil, *The Poems of Virgil*, "The Aeneid VI," p. 212 in vol. 13 of *Great Books of the Western World*.

[4]Smith, *op. cit.*, 20.

[5]*Loc. cit.*

[6]*Loc. cit.*

[7]*Loc. cit.*

[8]*Ibid.*, p. 21.

[9]*Ibid.*, p. 22.

[10]*Ibid.*, p. 21.

[11]*Loc. cit.*

[12]*Ibid.*, p. 24.

[13]Cleon L. Rogers, "The Gift of Tongues In the Post Apostolic Church." *Bibliotheca Sacra*, 122:141.

[14]*Ibid.*, p. 143.

[15]Smith, *op. cit.*, p. 17.

[16]Joseph Dillow, *Speaking In Tongues*, p. 46.

[17]Smith, *op. cit.*, pp. 17-18.

[18]*Ibid.*, p. 19.

[19]*Ibid.*, p. 20.

[20]George W. Dollar, "A Symposium on the Tongues Movement." *Bibliotheca Sacra*, 120:321.

CHAPTER TWO

[1]G. Abbott-Smith, *A Manual Greek Lexicon of the New Testament*, p. 480.

[2]Joseph Dillow, *Speaking In Tongues*, p. 5.

[3]Merrill F. Unger, *Unger's Bible Dictionary*, p. 357.

[4]*New International Version of the New Testament*, p. 260.

[5]Don W. Basham, *A Handbook on Holy Spirit Baptism*, pp. 24-25.

[6]Charles R. Smith, *Tongues In Biblical Perspective*, p. 52.

[7]Dillow, *op. cit.*, pp. 50-54.

[8]George W. Zeller, *God's Gift of Tongues*, p. 33.
[9]John G. Mitchell, *A Biblical Study of Tongues and Healing*, p. 15.
[10]Dillow, *op. cit.*, pp. 159-160.
[11]Radio Station KPDQ, Harvest Time Broadcast, October 29, 1977.

CHAPTER THREE

[1]John G. Mitchell, *A Biblical Study of Tongues and Healing*, p. 19.
[2]*Loc. cit.*
[3]Joseph Dillow, *Speaking In Tongues*, p. 59.

CHAPTER FOUR

[1]Merrill F. Unger, *Unger's Bible Dictionary*, p. 221.
[2]*Loc. cit.*
[3]James Orr, *The International Standard Bible Encyclopaedia*, Vol. 2, p. 710.
[4]*Loc. cit.*
[5]H. A. Ironside, *The First Epistle to the Corinthians*, p. 15.
[6]*Loc. cit.*
[7]Unger, *op. cit.*, p. 221.
[8]George E. Gardiner, *The Corinthian Catastrophe*, p. 11.
[9]*Ibid.*, p. 12.
[10]Unger, *op. cit.*, p. 221.
[11]Gardiner, *op. cit.*, p. 19.
[12]*Loc. cit.*
[13]Joseph Dillow, *Speaking In Tongues*, p. 46.

CHAPTER FIVE

[1]George E. Gardiner, *The Corinthian Catastrophe*, p. 19.
[2]*Ibid.*, p. 12.
[3]Charles C. Ryrie, *Balancing the Christian Life*, p. 13.

CHAPTER SIX

[1]George W. Zeller, *God's Gift of Tongues*, pp. 107-110.
[2]George E. Gardiner, *Tapes of a Conference*, tape 2.
[3]Gardiner, *The Corinthian Catastrophe*, p. 23.
[4]Charles R. Smith, *Tongues In Biblical Perspective*, pp. 13, 20.

[5]Joseph Dillow, *Speaking In Tongues*, p. 182.

[6]*Loc. cit.*

[7]Roy L. Laurin, *First Corinthians, Where Life Matures*, p. 203.

[8]Earl D. Radmacher, *Tapes of a Conference*, tape 1.

[9]Gardiner, *op. cit.*, p. 24.

[10]*Ibid.*, pp. 24-25.

CHAPTER SEVEN

[1]Ron Boydston, ed., *The Church Around the World*, Vol. 7, No. 10, p. 1.

[2]George E. Gardiner, *The Corinthian Catastrophe*, pp. 26-27.

[3]*Ibid.*, p. 28.

[4]Albert Barnes, *Notes On the New Testament*, Vol. on *I Corinthians*, p. 240.

[5]Joseph Dillow, *Speaking In Tongues*, pp. 52-53.

[6]*Ibid.*, p. 87.

CHAPTER EIGHT

[1]George E. Gardiner, *The Corinthian Catastrophe*, p. 33.

[2]Cf. chapter 5, note 3.

CHAPTER NINE

[1]George E. Gardiner, *The Corinthian Catastrophe*, p. 34.

[2]Roy L. Laurin, *First Corinthians, Where Life Matures*, p. 244.

[3]Joseph Dillow, *Speaking In Tongues*, pp. 127-29.

[4]Laurin, *op. cit.*, p. 246.

[5]Dillow, *op. cit.*, p. 132.

[6]*Ibid.*, pp. 95-164.

[7]George W. Zeller, *God's Gift of Tongues*, p. 78.

[8]Walter R. Bodine, *The Quotation By Paul From Isaiah Regarding Tongues*, p. 49.

[9]Dillow, *op. cit.*, p. 112.

[10]*Ibid.*, pp. 158-59.

[11]Chrysostom, *Homilies on First Corinthians*, XXIX, 1.

[12]Augustine, *Ten Homilies on the First Epistle of John*, VI, 10.

CHAPTER TEN

[1]Don W. Basham, *A Handbook on Tongues, Interpretation and Prophecy*, p. 35.

[2]Roy L. Laurin, *First Corinthians, Where Life Matures*, p. 249.

[3]Carl Pfeil, *Charismatic Concerns*, p. 35.

[4]George E. Gardiner, *The Corinthian Catastrophe*, p. 41.

[5]Joseph Dillow, *Speaking In Tongues*, p. 118.

CHAPTER ELEVEN

[1]Zane C. Hodges, "A Symposium on the Tongues Movement." *Bibliotheca Sacra*, 120:229.

[2]Joseph Dillow, *Speaking In Tongues*, p. 38.

[3]G. Abbott-Smith, *A Manual Greek Lexicon of the New Testament*, p. 17.

[4]George E. Gardiner, *Tapes of a Conference*, tape 5.

[5]Charles C. Ryrie, *The Role of Women In the Church*, p. 74.

[6]Dwight J. Pentecost, *The Divine Comforter*, p. 192.

CHAPTER TWELVE

[1]Joseph Dillow, *Speaking In Tongues*, p. 9.

[2]George E. Gardiner, *The Corinthian Catastrophe*, pp. 50-51.

[3]Dillow, *op. cit.*, p. 172.

[4]*Ibid.*, pp. 172-73.

[5]*Ibid.*, pp. 174-75.

[6]John P. Kildahl, *The Psychology of Speaking in Tongues*, p. 54.

[7]E. Mansell Pattison, "Speaking In Tongues and About Tongues," *Christian Standard* (February 15, 1964), p. 2.

[8]Gardiner, *op. cit.*, p. 54.

[9]John F. MacArthur, *The Charismatics*, pp. 175-76.

[10]Kildahl, *op. cit.*, p. 74.

[11]Gardiner, *op. cit.*, p. 55.

[12]Dillow, *op. cit.*, p. 178.

[13]*Ibid.*, pp. 178-79.

[14]Donald W. Burdick, *Tongues: To Speak or Not to Speak*, p. 65.

[15]*Ibid.*, pp. 60-61.

[16]Charles R. Smith, *Tongues In Biblical Perspective*, pp. 94-95.

[17]Dillow, *op. cit.*, pp. 167-71.

[18]*Ibid.*, pp. 187-90.

Bibliography

Abbott-Smith, G. *A Manual Greek Lexicon of the New Testament.* Edinburgh: T. & T. Clark, 1948. 512 pp.

Augustine. "Ten Homilies on the First Epistle of John." Translated by H. Browne. *The Nicene and Post-Nicene Fathers*, edited by Philip Schaff, vol. 7, first series. Grand Rapids, Michigan: Wm. B. Eerdmans Publishing Company, 1956.

Barnes, Albert. *Notes on the New Testament.* 27 vols.; Grand Rapids, Michigan: Baker Book House, 1960.

Basham, Don W. *A Handbook on Holy Spirit Baptism.* 8th ed., Springdale, Pa.: Whitaker House, 1974, 140 pp.

Basham, Don W. *A Handbook on Tongues, Interpretation and Prophecy.* Monroeville, Pennsylvania: Whitaker Books, 1971. 123 pp.

Basham, Don W. *The Miracle of Tongues.* Old Tappan, New Jersey: Fleming H. Revell Company, 1973. 127 pp.

Bauman, Louis S. *The Modern Tongues Movement Examined and Judged In the Light of the Scriptures and In the Light of Its Fruits.* Long Beach, Calif.: Alan S. Pearce, 1941. 35 pp.

Bellshaw, William G. "The Confusion of Tongues." *Bibliotheca Sacra*, 120:145-53, April-June, 1963.

Bierman, Bud, and John Stauffacher. "Ecstasy and Emptiness: The 1977 Charismatic Conferences in Kansas City and in Lausanne," *Faith For the Family*, Greenville, South Carolina: Bob Jones University Press. Vol. 5, Number 9, November, 1977.

Bodine, Walter Ray. *The Quotation By Paul From Isaiah Regarding Tongues.* Unpublished Master's Thesis: Dallas Theological Seminary, Dallas, Texas, 1966. 76 pp.

Boydston, Ron, ed. *The Church Around the World.* Vol. 7, No. 10. Wheaton, Illinois: Tyndale House Publishers, 1977.

Bruner, Frederick Dale. *A Theology of the Holy Spirit.* Grand Rapids, Michigan: William B. Eerdmans, Publisher, 1976. 390 pp.

Burdick, Donald. *Tongues: To Speak or Not to Speak.* Chicago: Moody Press, 1969. 94 pp.

Chrysostom, "Homilies on First Corinthians." Translated by T. W. Chambers. *The Nicene and Post-Nicene Fathers*, edited by Philip Schaff, vol. 12, first series. Grand Rapids, Michigan: Wm. B. Eerdmans Publishing Company, 1956.

Dillow, Joseph. *Speaking In Tongues.* Grand Rapids, Michigan: Zondervan Publishing House, 1975. 191 pp.

Epp, Theodore H. *Studies on Mature Christian Living.* Radio messages from Corinthians. Lincoln, Nebraska: Back to the Bible Publishers, 1952. 79 pp.

Epp, Theodore H., and John I. Paton. *The Use and Abuse of Tongues.* Lincoln, Nebraska: The Good News Broadcasting Association, 1963. 47 pp.

Feinberg, Charles Lee. *Habakkuk, Zephaniah, Haggai, and Malachi.* New York: American Board of Missions to the Jews, Inc., 1951. 150 pp.

Gardiner, George E. *Tapes of a Conference.* Bangor, Maine: Bangor Baptist Church, 1977. 6 tapes.

Gardiner, George E. *The Corinthian Catastrophe.* Grand Rapids, Michigan: Kregel Publications, 1974. 56 pp.

Godet, Frederick L. *Commentary on the First Epistle of St. Paul to the Corinthians.* 2 vols. Translated by A. Cusin. Grand Rapids, Michigan: Zondervan Publishing House, 1957.

Hay, Alexander Rattray. *What Is Wrong In the Church?* vol. 2, "Counterfeit Speaking In Tongues," Audubon, New Jersey: New Testament Missionary Union, (n. d.). 126 pp.

Hillis, Don W. *What Can Tongues Do For You?* Chicago: Moody Press, 1963. 48 pp.

Hoekema, Anthony A. *What About Tongue-Speaking?* Grand Rapids, Michigan: William B. Eehdmans Publishing Company, 1966. 161 pp.

Ironside, H.A. *Lectures on the Book of Acts.* New York: L. B. Printing Co., Inc., 1945. 651 pp.

Ironside, H.A. *Notes on the Minor Prophets.* New York: Loizeaux Brothers, 1947. 464 pp.

Ironside, H.A. *The First Epistle to the Corinthians.* New York: Loizeaux Brothers, Publishers, 1941. 564 pp.

Johnson, S. Lewis, Zane C. Hodges, Stanley D. Toussaint, and George W. Dollar. "A Symposium on the Tongues Movement," *Bibliotheca Sacra,* 120:224-233 (July-September, 1963) and 120:309-321 (October-December, 1963).

Kildahl, John P., *The Psychology of Speaking in Tongues.* New York: Harper and Row, 1972. 110 pp.

Laurin, Roy L. *First Corinthians, Where Life Matures.* Wheaton, Illinois: Van Kampen Press, Inc., 1954. 332 pp.

MacArthur, John F., Jr. *The Charismatics.* Grand Rapids, Michigan: Zondervan Publishing House, 1978. 224 pp.

Macaulay, J. C. *A Devotional Commentary on the Acts of the Apostles.* Grand Rapids, Michigan: Wm. B. Eerdmans Publishing Company, 1946, 278 pp.

McCone, R. Clyde. *Culture and Controversy, an Investigation of the Tongues of Pentecost,* Phiosdelphia and Ardmore, Pennsylvania: Dorrance and Company, 1978. 136 pp.

McGee, J. Vernon. *Talking in Tongues.* Whittier, California: Walker-Smith, Inc., 1966. 21 pp.

Miles, John. *Tongues.* Unpublished notes on I Corinthians 12:1-13. Grand Rapids, Michigan: (n.n.), (n.d.).

Mitchell, John G. *A Biblical Study of Tongues and Healing.* Portland, Oregon: Christian Supply Center, n.d., 24 pp.

Morgan, G. Campbell. *The Acts of the Apostles.* New York: Fleming H. Revell Company, 1924. 547 pp.

Morgan, G. Campbell. *The Corinthian Letters of Paul.* Old Tappan, New Jersey: Fleming H. Revell Compsny (n.d.), 275 pp.

New American Standard Bible. La Habra, California: Foundation Press Publications, publisher for the Lockman Foundation, 1971.

New International Version of the New Testament of the Holy Bible. Grand Rapids, Michigan: Zondervan Bible Publishers, 1973. 573 pp.

Orr, James. ed., *The International Standard Bible Encyclopaedia.* vol. 2, Grand Rapids, Mich.: Wm. B. Eerdmans Publishing Co., 1946.

Pattison, E. Mansell. "Speaking in Tongues and About Tongues." *Christian Standard,* February 15, 1964, p. 2.

Pentecost, J. Dwight. *The Divine Comforter.* Westwood, New Jersey: Fleming H. Revell, 1963. 256 pp.

Pfeil, Carl. *Charismatic Concerns.* Renton, Washington: Family Bible Fellowship Press, 1978. 43 pp.

Pritchard, James B. ed. *Ancient Near Eastern Texts.* 2 vols. Princeton, N. J.: Princeton University Press, 1955.

Radmacher, Earl D. *Tapes of a Conference.* Tulsa, Oklahoma: Tulsa Baptist Temple, 1972. 2 tapes.

Radmacher, Earl D. *Glossolalia.* Portland, Oregon: Western Conservative Baptist Seminary, 1972. 12 tapes.

Radmacher, Earl D. *Spiritual Gifts.* Portland, Oregon: Western Conservative Baptist Seminary, 1975. 4 tapes.

Redpath, Alan. *The Royal Route to Heaven, Studies in First Corinthians.* Westwood, New Jersey: Fleming H. Revell Company, (n. d.). 248 pp.

Rogers, Cleon L. Jr. "The Gift of Tongues In the Post Apostolic Church." *Bibliotheca Sacra,* 122:134-43, April-June, 1965.

Ryrie, Charles Caldwell. *Balancing the Christian Life.* Chicago:

Moody Press, 1969. 191 pp.

Ryrie, Charles Caldwell. *The Acts of the Apostles*. Chicago: Moody Press, 1961. 127 pp.

Ryrie, Charles Caldwell. *The Role of Women In the Church*. Chicago: Moody Press, 1970. 155 pp.

Smith, Charles R. *Tongues In Biblical Perspective*. Second edition; Winona Lake, Indiana: B M H Books, 1973, 141 pp.

Smith, Charles R. and C. Norman Sellers. *Biblical Conclusions Concerning Tongues*. Miami, Florida: Miami Bible College, (n. d.). 28 pp.

Souter, Alexander. *Novum Testamentum Graece*. London: E Typographe-Clarendoniano, 1910.

Swindoll, Charles R. *Tongues*. Portland, Oregon: Multnomah Press, 1981. 23 pp.

Thomas, Robert L. *Understanding Spiritual Gifts*. Chicago: Moody Press, 1978. 238 pp.

Unger, Merrill F. *The Baptizing Work of the Holy Spirit*. Findlay, Ohio: The Dunham Publishing Co., 1962. 147 pp.

Unger, Merrill F. *Unger's Bible Dictionary*. Chicago: Moody Press, 1957. 1192 pp.

Van Gorder, Paul R. *The Church Stands Corrected*. Wheaton, Illinois: Victor Books, a division of S P Publications, Inc., 1976. 156 pp.

Virgil. *The Poems of Virgil* translated by James Rhoades in *Great Books of the Western World*. vol. 13. Robert M. Hutchins, ed. Chicago: Encyclopedia Britannica, 1952.

Walvoord, John F. *The Doctrine of the Holy Spirit*. 1st Edition. Dallas, Texas: Dallas Theological Seminary, 1943. 301 pp.

Walvoord, John F. *The Holy Spirit at Work Today*. Chicago: Moody Press, 1973. 63 pp.

Wells, Bob. *All the Bible Says About Tongues*. Denver, Colorado: Accent Books, 1977. 128 pp.

Westcott, Brooke F. and Fenton J. Hort. *The New Testament In the Original Greek*. New York: The Macmillan Company, 1946 620 pp.

White, Douglas M. *Charismatic Research*. Fincastle, Virginia: Scripture Truth Book Company, 1978. 12 pp.

Zeller, George W. *God's Gift of Tongues*. Neptune, New Jersey: Loizeaux Brothers, 1978. 126 pp.

Subject Index

Scripture Index

(See also Table of Contents)